12 STORIES

12 STORIES

12 STORIES

Discovering the Truth Behind Our Stories

Korbin Farmer

ISBN: 9798640017380 (Paperback)
Library of Congress Control Number: 2020907742

Some names and details within this book have been changed to protect the privacy of those involved.

All bolded sections of verses indicate author's emphasis.

The views presented in this book are the author's own and do not necessarily reflect the views of any institution or organization that might be mentioned within this book.

Front cover design by Kalli Farmer.

Printed in the United States of America.
First Edition 2020

To all those who experienced loss during
the COVID-19 pandemic...

the loss of a job, the loss of a sport season,
the loss of a graduation,
or the tragic loss of a loved one...

this book is dedicated to you.

TABLE OF CONTENTS

INTRODUCTION

Think back to the days where you first began to learn to write. Now when I say write, I do not mean simply putting letters together to form words and words together to create sentences. Rather when did writing to you become a form of artistry? Or has it?

I remember my days in junior high and high school when I would spend countless hours sitting in a desk listening to lecture after lecture on writing structure, paragraph creation, author's voice, and the list continues. What did I learn from these lessons?

1. The English language was so complicated compared to other languages (still to this day I have no clue what a dangling participle is).
2. I was definitely not cut out to be an English major in college.
3. The best writers are those who throw away all the rules and just write from the heart... this is what I plan to do.

My writing is not going to follow the intro, body, body, body, conclusion format I was taught. Nor am I going to try to grab my audience's attention with a funny story or creative quote at the beginning of each chapter. For this book is not meant for entertainment. I am not writing to please my audience nor am I writing to even please myself. The reason I wrote what you are currently reading is due to a crazy idea being placed on the heart of a 15-year-old sophomore boy that only now manifested itself in the work that is this book.

In the past I would consider including more of how exactly this creation came to be. But through the years patiently meditating on the content of my writing, I recognized the only place my personal stories have in this book are when they are doing the job of pointing others to the Larger Story. Therefore, I am not going to bother trying to make this book easy to read by adding the "glitter" and colorful details I might have done for an essay in my high school AP English class.

If anything, I want this entire book to be marked as plagiarized because I admit what follows from here is not of my doing at all. Yes, the words and thoughts might be of my own making, but any results – mental, emotional, or spiritual – must be credited to the Lord I serve. Only He can use this book to its utmost potential and only His Spirit can make the hearts of all who read this (and of me writing) soft enough to be transformed by the however many pages I end up composing.

My prayer for this work is together we find... together we learn... what it means to write. For all of us have stories that need to be written and a Story that needs to be shared. And trust me when I say this – New York Times Best Sellers have nothing on this Story.

Anyone can type characters on a page, but what I hope sets this book apart from others is you, the reader, clearly sees the heart poured into each and every letter... because true literature doesn't start with the pen, it begins within.

-CHAPTER 1-

A STORY OF HUMILITY

Humility. When you hear this word, what comes to mind? Your favorite baseball player pointing to the sky after hitting a homerun? A performer directing the audience's applause to the orchestra rather than accepting it solely for herself? A student acknowledging the success of his research was due to the support of a great group around him? Whatever the case might be, most of us can form some sort of image.

But what about the other side of the coin? What about the negative connotations our society has placed on this word – and there are many. People who appear humble often find labels of weak, cowardly, and unfit placed upon them. They could be seen as ashamed of their achievement while also demeaning said success for others pursuing the same goal.

Consequently, we are taught from a young age to be prideful and self-centered. Let's face it – for all of us, our favorite topic of interest is ourselves. This makes any attempt at humility empty and fake. Perhaps this is why humility gets a bad rap – it is a trait going directly against what society stands for and thus is labeled as such.

Worse yet – we as humans are naturally prideful creatures. Therefore, acts of humility require us to go against our own instincts. All the while, pride creates in us an undue confidence in our own skills, accomplishments, positions, and possessions. It engulfs us daily.

Game, set, and match. Might as well stop there. Chasing after this trait of humility is hopeless if the whole world, including myself, is against me... right? Wrong. As followers of Christ we are called to die to ourselves and put on the likeness of God, which is righteousness and holiness of the Truth (Ephesians 4:24). And the truth is this – humility is a necessity of life. John 3:30 reads:

> *"He must become greater and greater, and I must become less and less."*

If we are going to grow at all in our faith and relationship with Christ, we must first and foremost learn to die to ourselves and become a new creation. This might not be news to some; but to others it is the most important thing you will hear or see all day. When we die to self, we can be raised to new life with Christ (Galatians 2:20).

Realize, however, we will never find ourselves or our story by our own means. We find ourselves when we lose ourselves for the sake of the Lord (Luke 9:24). Then, and only then, can humility enter the picture. For ultimately, humility stems from understanding who God is and who we are in Him.

This venture towards a humbler life is not easy. We will be fighting an uphill battle. But one thing I do have confidence in is that while our journey as Christians might be tough and troubling, it is all worth it in the end.

◊ ◊ ◊ ◊ ◊

Perhaps that was too fast a start? Let me slow it down then and bring us back to Sunday school story time...

One of my all-time favorite stories is the story from Joshua 5, when Israel comes to Jericho. Just after crossing the river Jordan, the Israelite army faces perhaps the most intimidating stronghold in the region. While it is not exactly known how tall the walls around the city were, I am confident the Israelites were not able to just build a ladder and scale the embankment. This was a fortified city meant to stand against forces far greater than what they possessed. Yet, Joshua, their leader, was not fazed by the challenge before him.

The walls would not withstand the power of God at work through His people. In a battle plan that could only be described as crazy, the people of Israel rushed over the fallen walls of Jericho in just a week's time. I'm sure many of you know the story – Joshua, the Ark of the Covenant, and 40,000 Israel warriors would march around the city for six days in complete silence. Then on the seventh day, the army marched around the city seven times, the priests blew their horns, the people shouted, and the rest is history (full story found in Joshua 6).

For those familiar with this story, you know it is an amazing picture of how the Lord works in remarkable ways. The wall before us might be tall and seem impenetrable; but with God, those walls can come crumbling down. The Battle of Jericho reveals to us that the enemies before us will not prosper against our Lord and I believe that can provide great comfort to us. I mean, who doesn't want to see obstacles before us in our walk vanish?

But how do we get from our current position, our current situation, to the place where we can see walls fall? Is there a five-step plan we need to commit to or a certain inspirational Bible verse app we need to subscribe to? Name the price and I will pay it if that means the Jerichos of my life disappear. Perhaps though, this is not the main lesson we should be taking from this remarkable account. Let's look deeper into the story of Joshua at Jericho...

> When Joshua was near the town of Jericho, he looked up and saw a man standing in front of him with sword in hand. Joshua went up to him and demanded, "Are you friend or foe?"
>
> "Neither one," he replied. "I am the commander of the LORD's army."
>
> At this, **Joshua fell with his face to the ground in reverence**. "I am at your command," Joshua said. "What do you want your servant to do?"
>
> The commander of the LORD's army replied, "Take off your sandals, for the place where you are standing is holy." And Joshua did as he was told.
>
> *Joshua 5:13-15*

Joshua, as he is about to take on the biggest battle of his military career to date, is approached by this Heavenly warrior who is about to present him with the "secret strategy" needed to conquer the stronghold before him. And what does the leader of Israel do? He falls flat on his face. With this encounter, Joshua provides us perhaps one of the most excellent examples of humility in the Old Testament.

The moment he realizes he is about to encounter a direct command from the Lord, Joshua willingly submits himself to even the one who is delivering the message. He doesn't grumble or argue. Rather he – the leader of an entire nation of people – refers to himself as a servant. The Heavenly authority instructs Joshua to do something and he does it. And Joshua does all this from a position of complete vulnerability.

Think about it... Joshua is flat on the ground, face in the dirt, defenseless to any sort of attack. Personally, I can relate this to when I would wrestle my sisters when I was younger. To win, I would constantly be moving, trying to have the high ground or, at least, a solid low athletic stance. If I found myself lying face down on my stomach, I was pretty much pinned no matter how much strength I exerted. I would be defeated. Yet this position of defeat was the chosen position of Joshua. He chose a position of complete surrender.

What became of this surrender? Seven days later, through the power of the Lord, Joshua would lead Israel over the fallen walls of the city that had stood between Israel and the promised land. Joshua's surrender led to a victory of Biblical proportions!*

Joshua's surrender was not a sign of weakness. Instead, it was a demonstration of humility that came from wisdom and understanding. Proverbs 11:2 states, *"Pride leads to disgrace, but with humility comes wisdom."* Though this was written well after Joshua lived, he understood this fact well. To achieve triumph over the situation which stood before him, he first had to realize Who it was that would guarantee the victory.

God wants us to play a part in His plans. When we face a Jericho-sized wall in our lives, God is more than willing and able to bring the wall down, especially if what He has promised to us stands behind the wall. Notice, however, Joshua still had a role to play in order to see success. In our lives, we still have a role to play. If God chooses to bring down the walls, we must recognize we still have the

---

* Quite literally.

responsibility to storm the city and battle the army that resides within.

But what happens if God chooses not to bring down the walls in our life? What happens if that temptation still stands? That break-up? That tough friendship? The broken family situation? The loss of a loved one? What happens in the times where it seems the walls before us are just being built higher? What happens is this – we must change our perspective. We serve a loving and powerful God who is able to use tales of tragedy as the opening chapter to an account of absolute triumph.

Perhaps God is allowing the external struggles in your life to grow because He is trying to tear down a wall you don't even know exists. Rather than changing your circumstances, God is trying to change your heart. For before God could conquer Jericho, God first had to conquer Joshua. Before God transforms your situation, He wants to tackle your soul. He has a game plan ready to share with you, but He needs your complete submission first.

We all have a fight that needs to be fought and a victory needing to be realized. As Ephesians 6 declares, this fight is not against flesh and blood but against spiritual forces unseen. One tactic of our enemy is to tempt us with pride that would leave us unable to submit to Christ. Pride leads us to believe we are capable of living without God.

I can find love myself.
I can make plans for myself.
I can obtain approval by myself.
I can achieve joy myself.
I can knock this "wall" down myself.

This is the opposite of what rings true of Joshua. Despite being a powerful leader, he knew the fight before him could not be won by his own strength. He humbled himself to the point he was literally as low as dirt. Instead of fighting with our chest held high, we need to begin in a position of complete submission to the will of the Lord. For one of the first steps in defeating pride in this fight we call life is admitting it naturally exists in our hearts and we need God's help to rid it from our lives.

From there, we can begin to identify the triggers and situations causing us to be prideful and march around them until God tears the walls of pride down. It might take 7 days or 7 years but persisting in God's plan produces results. It is an everyday endeavor, however. The fight is and will not be easy.

◊ ◊ ◊ ◊ ◊

Practically, what does humility look like in everyday life? In Philippians 2:3, Paul instructs us to "*[not] be selfish or try to impress others. Be humble, thinking of others as better than yourself.*" One of the first steps is to place others before yourself. It is not just living a selfless life – it is actually thinking of yourself less.

A humble person recognizes what lurks inside their heart and the sin that resides within better than what resides in the hearts of others. They see the shortcomings and the depravity within their own life yet grant others a benefit of doubt. They are able to extend grace to those who oppose them more easily. People of great humility are compassionate, empathetic, and servant-hearted. They give easily because they recognize how much has been given to them.

More importantly, apart from putting others before themselves, they have Christ placed as the center of their lives. Humility, contrary to popular belief, teaches us the world doesn't exist to glorify us... Earth does not revolve around us.

The reason of creation is to glorify the only Name worthy of receiving glory. All praise received is ultimately praise directed towards God the Father. Humility allows us to love Christ in everything we do because it opens our eyes to our desperate need for Him and His awesome sacrifice for us.

As it was once described to me, the mark of humility is JOY. Yes, this can mean joy in the sense of the great feeling produced inside our soul by the Holy Spirit. But it is also an acronym of how to approach life. We should be placing Jesus first, Others second, and Yourself third. This three-part formula is how we should carry ourselves through our everyday journeys.

A warning concerning humility: Scripture never commands us to never think of ourselves. It simply says to think of ourselves appropriately as God views us (see Romans 12:3). We should care for our own wellbeing as well as the wellbeing of others.

If we don't care for ourselves, we lose the ability to pour into the lives of other people. We must be cognizant of the health of our own faith, allowing for adequate times of rest for our spiritual well-being. True humility will help you avoid "burning out" of your faith.

Another mark of humility is the ability to admit mistakes. Today, especially for men, admitting fault or the need for assistance is a mark of weakness. As the mantra of Agent Gibbs from my favorite show NCIS even declares, "Rule #6, Never apologize, it's a sign of weakness." While I love this TV series, it misses the mark with this idea. Perhaps the greatest act of strength we can show as Christians is going up to someone and saying these three words – "I messed up." And if I had to add two more: "Forgive me."

Looking at the story of David, a man after God's own heart, shows us how important it is for us to humble ourselves and admit our mistakes. In Psalm 51, David was confessing his mistake directly to God in prayer...

> *Wash me clean from my guilt.*
> *Purify me from my sin.*
> *For I recognize my rebellion;*
> *it haunts me day and night.*
> *Against you, and you alone, have I sinned;*
> *I have done what is evil in your sight.*
> *Purify me from my sins, and I will be clean;*
> *wash me, and I will be whiter than snow.*
> *Forgive me for shedding blood, O God who saves;*
> *then I will joyfully sing of your forgiveness.*
> *Unseal my lips, O Lord,*
> *that my mouth may praise you.*
> *Psalm 51:2-4a, 7, 14-15*

I really wish I could include Psalm 51 to its entirety right there but knowing many of you reading this (and myself) would see a huge piece of Scripture and skip right over it – which is definitely not what I want to happen. So, if you are willing, I encourage you to go read all of Psalm 51 right now. Honestly, I would not even care if you just put down this book and started reading all of King David's story.

While I pray God will use my words to shape lives and eternities, I have the certainty the Bible has those credentials already so feel free to switch this book for your Bible at any time.

For those of you who are still continuing with me on this journey, let me get back on track. Psalm 51 was written by King David after committing adultery with Bathsheba and having her husband killed on the frontlines of war. Only after he is approached and rebuked by the Prophet Nathan does David recognize his sin. This psalm is David's outcry to God admitting his mistakes and asking for forgiveness.

A proud man would find it extremely difficult to say the prayer David did to the Lord. I mean this prayer not only admits guilt but shows David's dependence on the Lord and how powerless he is compared to the One he serves. In this moment David did not care how his words were going to be perceived because he was faced with true brokenness. He cared more about his heart condition than others' perception of him.

Now here's a question – what if we took after David?† What if we looked at our own hearts and our own mistakes and made Psalm 51 our prayer? And who could respond to these confessions and offer the forgiveness we need?

Enter Jesus.

Jesus offers a clear picture of humility through His birth, His life, and His death. The King of Kings, Lord of Lords, Son of God, ruler of all creation never once sought to lift Himself high. In all His encounters, He strived to bring glory to God the Father. Jesus did not merely associate with the rich or religious (as we might expect He would) but with the sick, poor, and low of society. He did not seek to be served rather He sought to serve (see Matthew 20:28). Even to the one who would betray Him, Christ still knelt to wash his feet.

The King of Kings entered the Holy City Jerusalem – not with a parade of trumpet sounds and celebration but on the back of a donkey. Then, less than a week later, Jesus carried out the greatest act of humility ever. Jesus was

---

† Not the rape and murder part, but the confession and repentance part.

10

wrongly accused, painfully tortured, stripped naked, and hung on two pieces of wood to die. Despite having the power to keep this from happening to Himself, our Savior persevered. He knew the plan God desired.

Jesus became nothing so that you and I could experience freedom.

He never insisted on His rights and privileges to be honored, understood, or viewed rightly, but He emptied Himself of His reputation. He was content taking on an ordinary human form. Jesus had lowliness of heart. And God puts a high price on the humility of the heart. He will honor those who trust Him with their hearts.

> *He humbled himself in obedience to God and died a criminal's death on a cross.*
> *Therefore, God elevated him to the place of highest honor and gave him the name above all other names,*
> *that at the name of Jesus every knee should bow, in heaven and on earth and under the earth,*
> *and every tongue confess that Jesus Christ is Lord, to the glory of God the Father.*
> *Philippians 2:8-11*

For us, Jesus is the perfect example of how we should approach everything we do. He had every reason to boast – His miracles, a sinless life, resurrection from death – but Christ never once boasted in Himself. Rather He displayed great humility to give all glory to His Father.

Personally, I truly discovered this trait of the Lord and the importance of it while working at a Fellowship of Christian Athletes (FCA) camp one summer. Typically at camp, I would be serving in a role as a huddle leader (counselor) but this particular time I was fulfilling a new role to me – intern. I was tasked with cleaning up after campers would leave an area, setting up playing fields before campers arrived, and pretty much doing whatever the camp director needed me to do – all the while my actions would go unannounced and unrecognized. Having served as a huddle leader many times before, I welcomed this change as an opportunity for personal growth.

As a leader I had direct access and influence on campers' lives, but my role as intern was meant to "prepare the stage" for others to speak into the lives of all the attendees. While this was a humbling experience in itself, this was not the most important thing God taught me at this camp.

The final night of camp arrived, and chapel service had just begun. I took my position high above the seats below in the sound booth to make sure this night ran smoothly. For those reading this who have ever been to a Christian camp before, you might recall the last night of camp always seems to be the most powerful. Everyone is engaged in worship just slightly more than the rest of the week, the speaker's message is laced with just a little more urgency, and there are usually a lot of tears of joy… and I mean a lot.

Even as intern, I would not escape the power found within this night.

God opened my heart and showed me while many people in the room were simply experiencing emotions, there was a far greater number truly encountering Jesus for the first time. The heart changes were real. This revelation brought tears to my eyes as I stood alone in the sound booth. But what happened next would bring me into the same position Joshua found himself in before approaching Jericho.

Previous camps I stood among the campers and was blessed with the privilege of counseling them through the moment they were in, but that night I was removed from the picture. My position could have easily been filled by someone else and this moment which was occurring before my eyes would still be happening. I was not needed.

God was and is still able to transform the lives of those around me without me and this night of camp revealed this fact to me. I needed God, but God did not specifically need Korbin Farmer. God was still God without me.

Once you realize this truth, you can't help but be overcome by humility. Because with this truth also comes the realization that despite us being nothing to God, He still desires to use us. How awesome is that? And honestly this is the message of the Gospel...

God created us and we turned away from Him, choosing our flesh over relationship with the Creator of the cosmos. Because of this, we find ourselves separated from our Father and deserving of death. BUT GOD, through His great love and mercy, set off on a divine rescue mission through His Son so the way back into community with Him may be restored. Jesus was crucified on a cross, thrown in a grave, and resurrected after three days, defeating death and taking our punishment away. What did we do in this? Absolutely nothing.

As Ephesians 2:8-9 states, *"God saved you by his grace when you believed. And you can't take credit for this; it is a gift from God. Salvation is not a reward for the good things we have done, so none of us can boast about it."* We are saved by grace through faith and when we realize this, we are truly humbled.

Take note, because this message right here is the most important thing you will read throughout this book. The message of the Gospel has more life-changing ability than anything else for there is nothing quite like this Good News. And if you feel like you have a good understanding of what this message entails, I challenge you to think again.

The Gospel is not just something we hear or read once and comprehend. Rather, it is a daily reminder of how God is all we need. We will never move on from the Gospel but simply move to a more profound understanding and appreciation of it. For our story begins and ends with humbly declaring this statement, "Christ is enough, and Christ alone can save."

Now we have the amazing opportunity to choose how to respond. Will we be prideful and live our life as we always have? Or will we admit our need for a Higher Power and seek to serve and glorify Him in all we do? This is the question we must answer every day. And it is this question I challenge you to consider as you continue reading this book.

JILL'S STORY

All throughout high school, I prided myself on how others saw me. I strived to be the best daughter to my parents I could be. I always followed the rules, tried my hardest in school, competed hard in sports, and did lots of community service. Having grown up in church, I also involved myself in church groups and sought to be the first to volunteer for things. This made me look polished around the edges. I just wanted to go above and beyond and make people proud of me, and it quickly became my identity and really the only thing I cared about.

It wasn't until I was challenged in my faith during various Christian camps that I began to question this identity. I realized that we are constantly falling short of the glory of God and there was nothing we could do on our own to change that. This was an extremely hard concept for me to wrap my head around. Had all that hard work I put forth to be seen as a leader and to upkeep my image gone to waste? Then I was revealed where I was so wrong.

No matter how hard I kept trying to be perfect, I will always miss the mark. But this is when the good news of the Gospel became real for me. Jesus died for my sins and failures and achieved the perfection I sought. He was calling me to lay down my failures at His feet and give my insecurities over to Him. Doing this made me feel like a weight was lifted off my shoulders.

I no longer had to work to please people in my life, for my work was to please my Father in Heaven. With this in mind, I also knew He was calling me to love others and continue to work at everything as if I was working for the Lord. This perspective today lights a fire in my soul to serve others. But now not so the world views me as a giving person, but so that I can bring glory to my God.

My calling is to serve and love others as Christ served and loved me. I am able to still hold these leadership positions in my life today, but it is not to show others how great a leader I can be. It is to glorify the Lord and allow His light to shine through my life. Instead of priding myself on how others saw me, I sought to humble myself to the will of my Lord.

Today my prayer is that I continue to show others His love through my actions and my positions. I hope to live my life where others seek to follow me as I follow and look to Jesus. And this won't be anything I do on my own. For God has shown me again and again that I need Him to give me the strength and courage to love others well. I seek to lay down my own desire to be known by the world and now seek to make Him known.

-CHAPTER 2-

A STORY OF INTEGRITY

Whenever I meet someone for the first time, I usually end up answering three questions. For those of you who may never earn the "privilege" to meet me (or as my sisters would say, who are blessed to never come across me), I will answer the questions for you now in the way I would if we found ourselves face to face.

Question 1: How tall am I?
4 foot, 30 inches.

Question 2: Where is your accent from?
Nowhere. I have a twin sister and when we were young, we had our own language which took me years to fully adapt out of. I got stuck with my "accent" because of that. So yes, siblings always mess everything up.

Question 3: What did you study at college?
Everything. I am a Philosophy and Mathematics Dual-Degree with a Communication Minor.

Why do I state these things? First, I think it is wise for you to have some knowledge as to where these words you are reading come from. Second, and more relevant to this chapter, I believe my two areas of study can offer us great insight as to what integrity is.

Two major terms discussed in Philosophy are *ethics* and *morality*. While these words are closely related, there are some differences we must understand concerning them of which I find it extremely difficult to define integrity without.

Ethics refers to the principles or beliefs by which a person lives. It is the standard of right and wrong someone holds. If a person is described to have good ethics, it means their beliefs of right and wrong line up with however another person or culture judges them.

Conversely, morality refers to the *lived* standard of right and wrong. It refers not to what someone says they believe is right or wrong but rather to what they actually do. Their actions are what take precedence when judging morality.

Combining these two ideas is where integrity enters the picture. To have integrity, in one sense, means to be whole and undivided.* Integrity then can be said to occur when one's ethics align with one's morality. It is actions correctly aligning with beliefs and words. To truly demonstrate this point, let me give you this thought experiment:

> Imagine I held a belief that it was right for me to steal everything from my friend Kevin, burn his room to the ground, and then kill him. You might describe me as having extremely bad ethics... I mean stealing, arson, and murder are all usually deemed unethical. Nevertheless, I am faced with two paths.

---

* Definitions of ethics, morality, and integrity adapted from Kenneth Boa's 2005 Commentary on Integrity on Bible.org.

Path 1: I really do not care what people or society say, so I decide to act on my belief.

Path 2: I am afraid of the penalties of acting on my beliefs so all I can bring myself to do is shoot Kevin with a nerf gun.

For Kevin's sake, and possibly for your sake, I bet everyone would hope I would choose the second path. But this would mean I would be a man of weak or no integrity. My morality (actions) did not align with my ethics (beliefs).

If integrity were the most important thing to me, option one would be the choice I should have made as this path would have preserved my integrity. Yes, this means Kevin dies and I probably earn a one-way ticket to federal prison but at least I kept my integrity! Right?

Hopefully you see a glaring issue with this thought experiment, because if you do not, then we are all in serious trouble.

The reason I proposed this is to demonstrate that before seeking integrity we must first take a step back to check our ethics. If we are lost ethically, seeking integrity would only provide detrimental consequences. If we do not figure out a good way to decide right from wrong, then there is no way we can pursue true integrity.

But how do we determine good ethics? How can we know the correct course of action? Unfortunately, philosophy only offers wild conjectures as to definite answers to these questions. Thankfully, a helpful guide comes from within my other field of study – mathematics!

One of the key ideas learned in any calculus class is the idea of taking the derivative of an equation. This process allows the mathematician to calculate the slope of a line tangent to a function or it can be used as a tool to approximate nonlinear functions locally with a linear function. How cool is that?!?! Not to mention, in many cases there are dozens of different methods you can use to arrive at the exact same answer. This, of course, just complicates the solving process even more! Got it? Good!

Time to graduate to the next level of calculus. Let's say we start with the tangent line (or the "answer") from the derivative question and we wish to know how it is we arrived at said result. With math, this is possible! Using a process called integration, or taking the integral, we use a variety of differing techniques to work the problem backwards to find the original function or the source.

Why do I mention this terrible thing known as math? Is it because I am trying to scare you into putting this book down and picking up a much more interesting book (like the Bible)?† Maybe... but, in reality, this idea of integration is the foundation of discovering integrity. It is the way we find the answer to the unanswerable question of good ethics philosophy left us.

If an etymologist were to explain the roots of the word integrity, they would tell us the word finds its origin in the Latin word *integer* which then produced the word "integrate." To integrate something means "to make whole" or "to be put together."‡ Integrity then could be defined as man being integrated – being made whole and pieced together.

This begs the question, how do we become integrated? Just like in math, we can go backwards to find the answer. Let us break down the problem that is ourselves to find the answer of integrity.

---

† I recognize some of you reading this might find math more interesting than say Leviticus, but hopefully my point on the matter still comes through. Also, if you like numbers so much, just go read the book after Leviticus.
‡ Paraphrased from Merriam-Webster Dictionary.

We will begin by looking past the external walls and masks we put up in our lives to protect ourselves and look at the internal. Like many of the topics that will be discussed in this book, integrity begins with a decision you make in your heart, allowing the person you are on the outside to match the convictions have on the inside. This is how man should be because this is how our Creator is.

In the beginning, God created...

God created us to be perfect and holy like He is perfect and holy. He created us to be whole and complete as He is whole and complete. He created us to be vessels of praise and worship for He is worthy of praise and worship. In God alone the source of integrity is found. We can develop good ethics because God is fully good. We can become complete because God offers fullness through Christ. God is the solution to the "math problem" that is integrity.

Sadly, though, in life we are like the majority of people who would take my Advanced 400-level Calculus class... we are and will be failing. There is no way for us to uphold God's standard of integrity because we are broken. We have disintegrated our own lives by our lack of ethics and morality.

Malachi 3:6 reads, *"I the Lord do not change"* (NIV). This assures us God's constant character allows us to fully trust in Him. But we also know we do change... a lot. God is to integrity as we are to a concept we know all too well – sin.

Returning to our trustworthy etymologist, "sin" has been defined from a Greek concordance referring to the act or state of missing the mark. To sin means to be in error which was commonly used to describe missing the bullseye in archery. But apart from having a dictionary definition of sin, do we know what this word means?

James 4:17 reads, *"So whoever knows the right thing to do and fails to do it, for him it is sin"* (ESV). If we truly understood sin, then we would be brought to our knees in its presence. We would be in tears when we fall short of God's standard. We would be doing whatever we could to keep ourselves and others pure. But we don't. Why? There are two possible reasons:

First, as a society we have become immune to sin's effects – namely we lack conviction of our sin. We are being desensitized. Don't believe me? Just watch the news.

From a country in political turmoil to mass shootings happening every other week, the world we live in is laced with horrific deeds. Just one of these events should be enough to spur us, the Church, to action, but we much rather sit around doing miniscule tasks that hold no eternal significance. News flash – mindlessly playing video games for hours on end saves no one!

Now let me make this a little more personal, because it is so easy to recognize someone else's sin and neglect our own...

As Americans in general we are very stuck-up, stubborn, prideful, and to be honest, flat out lazy – all of which are considered sin in the Lord's eyes. We lie to others to protect our self-image. We gossip to make ourselves appear dominant. We refuse to show weakness because we might be labeled as soft or needy. At least, these are a few examples from my own past.

We have become so complacent with our sin that we don't even view it as sin anymore. We are sinning without realizing it or labeling it as sin. I mean men, how is looking at a video of naked women on our phones while mastur-bating wrong? And who cares if the speed limit is 35, the flow of traffic is 45. Should I continue?

Are you starting to see the problems? How can we know what sin is if we can't even identify it in our own lives?

The second reason we no longer feel convicted by our sins is that we have lost sight of the cross. We have replaced what the cross stands for with what it looks like. We are perfectly fine with wearing a cross on our necks, but we will avoid bearing a cross on our backs.

Christ lived a perfect life because God knew that we could not. No matter how many good deeds we do, we all have sinned and fallen short of His standards. Therefore, He who knew no sin, bore the weight of every terrorist attack, every porn video, and every speeding violation so that we might know God!

Sin is a very serious issue and it is time we stop ignoring it. However, because of Christ, we have hope amidst the seriousness of sin. We have redemption because of a wonderfully mysterious thing called grace.

We will mess up and God knows this. That is why the message of the Gospel exists in the first place! Grace covers us for the times we fall into old ways, for all the times we lack integrity, and for when we fail to truly reflect the goodness of Christ. This grace which saves us is also the same grace that will shape us into the men and women we have been called to be.

In the end, we become what our desires make us. If we desire this world, we will continue in our sinful ways ultimately paving our own path towards destruction; however, if we yearn for God, integrity in a Biblical sense becomes possible.

As we discover the character of our awesome God, we will understand how broken we are. But as our focus shifts to the grace of our Lord and Savior, we recognize even though we might feel broken and undone, Christ is making us whole. As we see in 2 Corinthians 12:9, *"[His] grace is sufficient for [His] power is made perfect in weakness"* (NIV).

Recognizing this notion of grace then allows us to truly begin to discover the possibility of integrity for it opens us up to say one of the most powerful prayers we can ever declare – "God, show me myself."

When we ask the Lord to reveal to us who we are, we obtain new insights into who it is we were actually created to be. We know with this declaration we are laying down our lives and allowing the Spirit of the Lord to take root in our hearts.

Many times, however, discovering who we are is a whole lot tougher than just saying a prayer. And past that, staying true to who we are in Christ is equally as difficult. This is why integrity is of such high value! We must remain true to our commitment to faith from our acceptance of Christ to the day God calls us home. We must allow God to reveal more of Him to us in our pursuit of righteousness. All too often, He will do this through the trials we face...

◊ ◊ ◊ ◊ ◊

The book of Daniel opens by introducing five main characters – Daniel (duh), King Nebuchadnezzar, and three friends: Shadrach, Meshach, and Abednego. These three friends, along with Daniel, faced a great decision concerning whether or not their relationship with God was worth upholding. Throughout their story, there existed many opportunities to have played the victim and conformed to societal standards; however, they remained faithful. They decided to declare themselves to be men of God – and the King and his staff knew it.

After enduring a massive test of their integrity and commitment, Shadrach, Meshach, and Abednego faced the fire – literally. King Nebuchadnezzar, full of himself, erected a 90-foot tall idol for his people to worship... but some men refused.

> Nebuchadnezzar flew into a rage and ordered that Shadrach, Meshach, and Abednego be brought before him. When they were brought in, Nebuchadnezzar said to them, "...I will give you one more chance to bow down and worship the statue I have made... but if you refuse, you will be thrown immediately into the blazing furnace. And then what god will be able to rescue you from my power?"
>
> Shadrach, Meshach, and Abednego replied, "O Nebuchadnezzar, we do not need to defend ourselves before you. If we are thrown into the blazing furnace, the God whom we serve is able to save us. He will rescue us from your power, Your Majesty. But even if he doesn't, we want to make it clear to you, Your Majesty, that we will never serve your gods or worship the gold statue you have set up."
>
> *Daniel 3:13-18*

Whether or not God were to save them, these three men were determined to live out their faith. Neither the situation nor the possibility of a poor outcome would cause them to waiver in the commitment they made. They knew who they were and, more importantly, whose they were. God was going to do what was best for His glory, so they decided to see the path they were walking through to the end.

Now if you are familiar with this story, you must know the ending. Nebuchadnezzar ordered the men thrown into the furnace (which was heated to seven-times its original heat). While it seems like a hopeless situation – the end of the road – God was about to heat things up even more.§

> *Shadrach, Meshach, and Abednego, securely tied, fell into the roaring flames. But suddenly, Nebuchadnezzar jumped up in amazement and exclaimed to his advisers, ... "I see four men, unbound, walking around in the fire unharmed! And the fourth looks like a god!"*
>
> *Then Nebuchadnezzar came as close as he could to the door of the flaming furnace and shouted: "Shadrach, Meshach, and Abednego, servants of the Most-High God, come out! Come here!" ... then the high officers, officials, governors, and advisers crowded around them and saw that the fire had not touched them.*
>
> *... Nebuchadnezzar said, "Praise to the God of Shadrach, Meshach, and Abednego! He sent his angel to rescue his servants who trusted in him. They defied the king's command and were willing to die rather than serve or worship any god except their own God... There is no other god who can rescue like this!"*
>
> *Daniel 3:23-29*

Staying true to the path God called them to walk not only allowed for Shadrach, Meshach, and Abednego to experience a divine presence, but it also opened the hearts of those around them. God transformed a horrific situation into one of miraculous transformation through the boldness of three ordinary men.

---

§ I grew up in a household were dad jokes were the norm... so sorry but not sorry.

Shadrach, Meshach, and Abednego said they had faith and truly lived it out! What about you? If you call yourself a Christian, do you have the integrity to be able to go through the fires of life and remain true to who God is calling you to be?

These fires could be the temptation to pursue societal norms to hardships you are facing that are creating a sense of doubt to persecution from others because of your beliefs. Whatever the case, will you remain rooted in faith?

First and foremost, this is only achieved by relying upon God. He knows of the trial you are going through and He alone knows what the desired outcome is. Through the tough times, God is wanting to mold us into mighty warriors for His cause – He wants to create men and women above reproach. These trials and tests are meant to purify your faith, creating in you a genuine hope and authentic conviction.

Just as fire purifies gold, so also do the fires of life reveal the true persons of faith. And through this process, God brings those who remain strong the praise, glory, and honor (1 Peter 1:7). For this saying is trustworthy – our character is formed in the fire... it showed true for Daniel's three friends and it certainly will hold true for us.

So, when times get tough, do not fall away in timidity and fear, but boldly proclaim the name of Jesus. He will be with you in the fire and He will comfort you in seasons of trouble for there is power in His name. And with this truth comes the most important aspect of Biblical integrity – it is relying on God in all aspects of your life. You are fulfilling your role as a follower of Christ through the good and bad times of life, taking after God and not changing based on circumstances.

Furthermore, with integrity comes an element of consistency. Who you are in private is who you are in public. Yes, it is possible to live one life publicly and another life privately – but that is not integrity. We are to live with consistency in public and in private, because our Father "sees what is done in secret" (Matthew 6:4).

Men and women of integrity make it a priority not to be living two different lives. They are the same Saturday night as they are Sunday morning as they are midday Monday. When any sort of idol is put before them, they refuse to worship it. This could mean not bowing down to peer pressure, schoolwork, sport, or even religion itself.

Integrity as defined above means to be fully integrated, to be complete. Those seeking to live as such will not compromise their faith for things that will disintegrate them – they flee sin and pursue love, joy, and peace. People of great Biblical integrity are those who find their ethical code in the Word of God. As James 1 states, they are doers of the Word, not mere hearers.

The Message Translation of Scripture paraphrases this idea of consistency well:

> We refuse to wear masks and play games. We don't maneuver and manipulate behind the scenes. And we don't twist God's Word to suit ourselves. Rather, we keep everything we do and say out in the open, the whole truth on display, so that those who want to can see and judge for themselves in the presence of God.
>
> *2 Corinthians 4:2*

Are you wearing a mask? Are you hiding behind others' judgements or are you seeking to be a light for those living in darkness, day and night?

If you want to truly test this question, go up to a close brother or sister in Christ and ask – *am I showing Christ regardless of my audience, regardless of my situation, or am I letting my surroundings shape my actions and beliefs?* Trust me, if the person you ask this question to is a true follower of Christ, they will give you an answer perhaps you do not want to hear... or hopefully for most of you, they will just affirm you are walking the right path and should stay the course.

Finally, keep your word! If you say you are going to do something and that thing conforms to the will of God, then do it!**

Recognize when we as Christians fail to keep our word, we are not just failing ourselves, but we are failing others as well. Even failing to keep your word to yourself could affect those around you. If you tell yourself you will complete such and such task and stop before its completion because "no one will know," not only are you cutting yourself short, but you declare to your Lord integrity is not a trait you truly value – you are declaring you know best.

Psalm 15 finishes by saying those who are worthy of the Lord's presence are those who "keep their promises even when it hurts."†† It means we make a promise and keep it no matter what the cost financially, physically, or emotionally. It is valuing conviction over convenience.

Will we fail at this? As I wrote earlier – yes, of course. But does that mean we should not seek to work at this ideal with our whole heart? By no means! In this life, we will never achieve perfection. But at the very least, there should be progress towards the upward call of God in Christ. And when we fail, God provides us grace.

Pay close attention to your behavior and belief. Only when they are aligned is integrity found. And as the account of Shadrach, Meshach, and Abednego revealed to us,

---

** Reference Matthew 5:37.
†† Psalm 15:4b

staying true to what God has called us to allows for the opportunity of salvation – first from our fiery furnace, then others from theirs.

MITCHELL'S STORY

As I have grown up in the church and have experienced more and more life, I have come to grips with the importance of integrity as a follower of Jesus Christ. At the beginning of my freshman year at college, my integrity was tested in a great way.

Preseason for volleyball began and my team started off right away by spending copious amounts of time together. I had, for some strange reason, the expectation that since I was going to a private Christian university, I would be playing volleyball with a bunch of other believers. Or, at the very least, they would be understanding and respectful about my faith. After spending just 20 minutes with the team, I realized that my expectations were terribly wrong.

As disappointed as I felt in the moment, I felt the Holy Spirit rush to the scene and remind me of my purpose identifying this as my mission field. So, I slowly and carefully started taking conversations with my teammates to the next level. I took one on one opportunities to ask about their stories and their faith. Over time, a great amount of trust and relationships grew between us. Through listening, I recognized that they were longing for something and did not know what it was. So, I began introducing them to Jesus. This is when everything started to take a turn.

The guys had started to realize some things about my behaviors, or lack of behaviors. I did not drink with them, I did not smoke or vape with them, and I did not engage with girls in the ways that they did. This arose two things in them: questions and a passion to bring me down.

My teammates sought to understand what I understood as truth. They wanted to understand my righteousness, without understanding my Jesus. This made things difficult. It was hard for them to understand why I would be saving myself for marriage, when they did not believe in a God who created sex to be had between a man and a woman in the covenant relationship of marriage. These questions they would ask were brought to me with a fire and passion that I had never seen before. They were not trying to prove Scripture wrong or disprove Jesus, they just wanted me to mess up. There was a desire for me to say and do the wrong thing.

My teammates desired for me to act differently than how I was talking. They wanted to tear down my integrity. I came to the crossroads. My sinful nature said it would be so easy to run with them, but the Spirit in me said to run with endurance. So, I patiently waited on God and sought to persevere during this persecution.

Upholding my integrity was difficult. For my words and my actions begged for integrity. I needed to be in line with Scripture. Constant meditation on the Word of God was crucial for me and my witness to my teammates. In this time, I learned how to lean on Christ's strength and His grace, which made me realize that showing integrity was not so hard. In fact, God began to use my integrity and my faithfulness to transform three of my teammates' lives within the first two months of school.

Through this experience I was revealed a great lesson that our integrity as believers has an effect on the non-believers around us. And God can, and often will, use it for salvation.

-CHAPTER 3-

A STORY OF TRANSFORMATION

Rock, paper, scissors, PUNCH! If you are unfamiliar with this game, then consider yourself lucky. Unfortunately for me, I know this twisted version of a childhood classic all too well (and I have had bruises to remind me of it). Let me explain before you are too confused...

One of the greatest moments of every week for me when I am at college is having the opportunity to do a small group Bible study with some of my closest guy friends on campus.* Together we spend hours upon hours discussing how God has been impacting our lives to diving into various books of Scripture to confessing sins and shortcomings to one another to making random road trips to Chick-fil-a. Pretty much we do a bit of everything. But one activity sticks out to me we do which I would venture to say most (if not all) Bible studies do not participate in. This is playing a violent round of rock-paper-scissors.

The object of this game, like most, is to not lose. For if you lose, you get punched in the arm. Very simple rules

---

* We have called this group anything from Omelets & Jesus to The Bible Studlies to the Lowercase Kings.

with very real pain. How did we start this? I have no idea. Why did we do it? Once again, I have no answer. Perhaps it is due to the fact of us being a group of 21-year-old football and basketball players with a few powerlifters and wrestlers mixed in. Or maybe it was because people can make stupid decisions in college and this just happened to be one of ours. Whatever the case, despite how much "fun" we had with this game, we haven't played it in a while.

This of course brings about another question – why did we stop? To this I can only offer a well-educated guess. In my opinion, we grew in maturity by recognizing the importance of our fellowship with each other and came to the realization our time could be spent in much more beneficial ways – both spiritually and physically. And since we've halted this unique identifier of our group, we have experienced more in-depth conversation and study.

During one of our more recent times together, my friend RC decided to lead a discussion on the meaning of names. To me, while all our Bible studies together are great, this particular one holds a special place in my heart. Not only did RC take the time to brilliantly guide us through the story of Jacob[†], but he went the extra mile and gave us a small personalized printout as to what each of our names meant and how our names actually tied into pieces of our characters. For example, my name Korbin Alan Farmer, he broke down as such:

Korbin – raven, man with a raucous tone of voice
Take out the negative connotation and raucous can simply mean loud and commanding, which at points is exactly what a wild group of college

---

[†] Jacob is first introduced in Genesis 25, but his life story spans many chapters of Genesis.

guys needs. And just as the ravens who fed Elijah sought to serve God, so do you try daily.

Alan – harmony, stone, fair, handsome

Do I even need to explain handsome?

Farmer – cultivator of the ground

We have the opportunity to be planting seeds of faith and hope in people's life, and together with this group that is exactly what we set out to do.

This is just a mere summary of what he actually gave me, but hopefully you kind of get the point and perhaps like me you find this gift to be extremely thoughtful.

But the best part of this gift RC gave to me is that it got me thinking deeply about what is behind a name. The results of my reflection are what this chapter is all about. For just as RC took something as simple as a name and transformed it into a great testimony of how God defines us, so will I try to take you all on a journey to discover that even in the small things can exist moments of great transformation and meaning.

◊ ◊ ◊ ◊ ◊

The story of Jacob has always been one which sparks great interest to me. From what we know of Jacob's youth, he was a liar, cheater, and constantly sought self-satisfaction rather than seeking to serve or bring glory to the God of his father.

Yet despite these parts of Jacob's life, Exodus through Revelation we see God refer to Himself as the God of Jacob. Not to mention, it would be Jacob who God chose to build His chosen people and nation from. How did Jacob go from cheating his way into "prosperity" to be a man highly

favored by the Creator of the Cosmos? Let's pick up the
story in Genesis 32 to discover a reason...

After fleeing from his brother Esau and then living
decades apart from him fearing for his own life, Jacob
decides to take a risk to seek redemption. Having decided it
was time to face the consequences of his past, Jacob packed
up his family and began to make the journey home to face
his brother. Late one night on the trip, Jacob was left alone
when he encountered a strange figure:

> This left Jacob all alone in the camp, and a man
> came and wrestled with him until the dawn began
> to break. When the man saw that he would not
> win the match, he touched Jacob's hip and
> wrenched it out of its socket. Then the man said,
> "Let me go, for the dawn is breaking!"
>
> But Jacob said, "I will not let you go unless you
> bless me."
>
> "What is your name?" the man asked.
>
> He replied, "Jacob."
>
> "Your name will no longer be Jacob," the man told
> him. "From now on you will be called Israel,
> because you have fought with God and with men
> and have won."
>
> "Please tell me your name," Jacob said.
>
> "Why do you want to know my name?" the man
> replied. Then he blessed Jacob there.
>
> *Genesis 32:24-29*

If my friend RC was to break down what Jacob's name
meant, he would include something about how it translates
to "heel grabber." Not very appealing, right? However,

throughout Jacob's life he lived up to the expectation of what a "heel grabber" would do and be.

Think about it – if you are chasing someone and trying to impede their progress, you might do so much grabbing their heel from behind. This not only slows or stops the other person but could in fact cause damage to them. This is exactly how Jacob acted for many years of his life; he inflicted damage onto those around him (especially his twin Esau).

The night Jacob wrestled with God marks a watershed event in Jacob's journey. For the longest time, Jacob sought to meet his wants and needs by his own strength until he was faced with an adversary he cannot defeat – God. When the Lord asks Jacob what his name is, Jacob gives perhaps the most difficult answer of his life. Jacob told the truth.

In the past, Jacob responded to this very same question with deception. But when face to face with God, he accepts his name (and with that, his past and character) as his own. Jacob responded to the Man he wrestled with all night with the truth of who he is. He is a "heel grabber" ... a man who has cheated his way to where he currently is. How does God respond to this revelation? With a blessing.

God recognizes Jacob's name is how people have identified him and perhaps even labeled him, but to God "Jacob" was not how he was to be defined. It was this night God gave Jacob the name Israel. More importantly God gave Jacob a new identity.

No longer was Jacob to be known by the treasons of his old self, but by the promise God made (and kept). The promise to make him into a great nation. And this story is not exclusive to Jacob, for the same result is available to each of us.

Our names, our pasts, our reputations might appear set in the eyes of the world, but when we truly encounter our

Creator, we can and will change. For our name might explain us, but it is our Father who defines us.

When we come to this realization, things will never be the same. A new light should come to our eyes and a new swag to our step. In fact, for Jacob, he literally started walking differently after his encounter with God since his hip was wrenched out of socket. While I'm not sure Jacob was walking with swagger, he was at least living with a new perspective on life.

This is shown in the very next chapter of Genesis when Jacob was able to reconcile his relationship with Esau. No longer did Jacob need to con his brother for Jacob had access to a new source of provision.

Jacob encounters God → things change.

Of course, Jacob is not alone in this paradoxical story. Fast forward to a story in John 4, we see yet another story of miraculous transformation. Yes, for you Bible trivia loving experts, I am of course referring to the women at the well.

> *Soon a Samaritan woman came to draw water, and Jesus said to her, "Please give me a drink."*
>
> *The woman was surprised, for Jews refuse to have anything to do with Samaritans. She said to Jesus, "You are a Jew, and I am a Samaritan woman. Why are you asking me for a drink?"*
>
> *Jesus replied, "If you only knew the gift God has for you and who you are speaking to, you would ask me, and I would give you living water."*
>
> *"But sir, you don't have a rope or a bucket," she said, "and this well is very deep. Where would you get this living water? And besides, do you think you're greater than our ancestor Jacob, who*

gave us this well? How can you offer better water than he and his sons and his animals enjoyed?"

Jesus replied, "Anyone who drinks this water will soon become thirsty again. But those who drink the water I give will never be thirsty again. It becomes a fresh, bubbling spring within them, giving them eternal life."

"Please, sir," the woman said, "give me this water! Then I'll never be thirsty again, and I won't have to come here to get water."

"Go and get your husband," Jesus told her.

"I don't have a husband," the woman replied.

Jesus said, "You're right! You don't have a husband— for you have had five husbands, and you aren't even married to the man you're living with now. You certainly spoke the truth!"

...The woman said, "I know the Messiah is coming—the one who is called Christ. When he comes, he will explain everything to us."

Then Jesus told her, "I AM the Messiah!"

The woman left her water jar beside the well and ran back to the village, telling everyone, "Come and see a man who told me everything I ever did! Could he possibly be the Messiah?" So the people came streaming from the village to see him....

Many Samaritans from the village believed in Jesus because the woman had said, "He told me everything I ever did!" When they came out to see him, they begged him to stay in their village. So he stayed for two days, long enough for many more to hear his message and believe. Then they said to the woman, "Now we believe, not just because

of what you told us, but because we have heard
him ourselves. Now we know that he is indeed the
Savior of the world."

John 4:7, 9-18, 25-30, 39-42

This Samaritan woman set out to fetch water in the middle of the day because she did not want to face the shame that came with facing other people. Little did she know she was about to encounter the one person who would transform her story from one of shame to one of remarkable grace.

Jesus, who was alone at the time, knew His mission was one which would forever alter the course of world history; and what did He choose to do with His time? He sought to meet with a woman who society labeled as a slut and whore. because to Him changing the world meant transforming the lives of those who lived in the world. He knew this woman came to Jacob's Well for water, but He intended this moment to be used for so much more.

The Son of God went against societal expectations and had a conversation with this woman during which He revealed her messy past. Seeing this Man before her was no ordinary man, this woman responded not out of offense like many of us would, but rather out of curiosity and acceptance. She knew her life was a complete wreck, but also accepted that this Man could offer her something to finally quench the thirst she'd been experiencing.

Jesus laid out her story in a manner of great gentleness, care, and love. This allowed the woman the opportunity to learn the greatest truth ever.

How about you? If your past – mistakes and all – were laid out before you, could you respond like the Samaritan woman did? For the longest time, I'm not sure I could have.

My past is marked with so many sins and failures that I have tried to cover up in order to (what I believed at the time would) protect myself. I mean if someone were to discover all I ever did wrong, and they knew I called myself a Christian, how would those things in conjunction ever bring people to God? And that is where I found myself vastly mistaken.

Like John 4 shows, God is not afraid of using our dirt to fulfill His plan in other peoples' lives. In fact, many times God chooses to use the filth and grime of our stories in order to bring Him the most glory. As 2 Timothy 1:8-9 states, *"Therefore, do not be ashamed of the testimony about our Lord... but share in suffering for the gospel by the power of God, who saved us and called us to a holy calling, not because of our works but because of his own purpose and grace"* (ESV). We have a story, a testimony, God has given us in order to show others the power of the Gospel at work.

When we show and tell others about how perfect we are and spend energy covering up our weaknesses, we aren't doing the Lord's work but the work of the devil. The Samaritan woman recognized this and came clean to her entire city.

Because of her authentic passion for bringing people to Jesus, to a man she only just met, the entire city came to know the Messiah. Realize however, this passage clearly states that it was not the woman's actions which saved the village but her obedience to bring people to the Lord. She knew God was and is more capable to transform the hearts and minds of people than she would ever be.

We too must have this perspective. In order for transformation to happen in the lives of those around us, we must come to realize it is only God who has the power to impact a soul for eternity. And even before we can see transformation happen in those around us, we must allow it to occur in our own life. We must be willing to surrender to God our full self, from our highlight reels to our behind the scenes. Therefore, when our friends and family look at us, they no longer see who we were, but rather they see our Savior shining through us.

If you believe you are in a place where this is not possible because you have too much going on in your life you think is not pleasing to God, then throw some water in your own face and wake up! God didn't begin wrestling with Jacob when Jacob started to sort out the chaos in his own life nor did Jesus meet with the woman at the well after she prayed a prayer of repentance. No! We serve a Lord that desires us now! This means no matter how deep in mud we might be, God is coming after us! But we must be willing to listen.

No matter what you have done, come to Jesus how you are. Realize however, if you truly seek to encounter God, then you are not going to stay how you were. Just look at the examples throughout Scripture illustrating this:

> Saul was a murderer of Christians before encountering God. Afterwards he becomes Paul - one of the greatest missionaries this world has ever seen who wrote a majority of the books in the New Testament.
>
> Peter had denied Christ three times during the week of Jesus's crucifixion. Peter then reencounters his Lord and preaches the first evangelical message during which 3,000 people were saved.
>
> Elijah was suicidal and burnt out after being threatened by Jezebel. He encounters God through a still small voice reminding him he is not alone. Elijah goes onto perform many miracles in God's name.

David broke half of the Ten Commandments in one incident. God sends Nathan to encounter David during this troubling time and David repents getting to experience God's forgiveness like never before.

Gomer had prostituted herself out to the highest bidder. She encounters God's unwavering commitment to her through the actions of her husband Hosea, leaving us with one of the greatest pictures of redemption in Scripture.

Lazarus was dead. He encounters God and he finds new life in more ways than one.

And this list continues. For when things are going terribly wrong, instead of viewing the situation as the end of your story, view it as a call to encounter, or perhaps rediscover, the love and grace God offers. Just as you read above:

Samaritan woman encounters God → things change.

Fast forward one more time with me to a few chapters later in the book of John. In John 9, we meet yet another man who was transformed by the power of God at work. In this encounter, a man who was born blind crosses paths with Jesus and His disciples. What happens next, I guarantee this man did not see coming‡...

Jesus spits on the ground before him making mud. He then advances to take this mud and smear in onto the eyes of the blind man instructing him to go wash it off in the pool of Siloam. Immediately the man could see! His neighbors and others later recognized him as the blind beggar and took this changed man to the Pharisees. In the tradition of

---

‡ Pun intended.

the Pharisees, they freaked out. It was the Sabbath and they believed no healing should occur on this holy day. They sought out Jesus to rebuke him.

The formerly blind man did not play into the antics of the Pharisees and simply told his story to those who would listen. He was blind when he encountered Jesus, but now he could see. No one was going to talk him out of that story.

Even to the unbelief of his own parents, this man knew where he had been and where he was now were two different places. He knew he had set out that morning to beg for money only to find himself given the gift of sight. He encountered Jesus and he was going to tell this story regardless if anyone was willing to listen or not.

I encourage you to read this full story for yourself because I bet you will be able to see a lot more in this story than I just included.§ For now, I believe this encounter with Jesus sheds light on one key piece of truth this chapter is missing – Transformation can happen whenever and wherever to whoever. God's grace is not limited to church, summer camps, or nights of revival.

John 3:16 reads, as many of you might know, "For God so loved **the world**...". God's love, and hence His transforming power, is not just limited to those who grew up in church or to those wealthy enough to afford a week's stay at a Christian camp, but it is available to ALL!

Blind beggar encounters God → things change.

Every story in this chapter, in addition to yours and mine, all have a few key things in common. Firstly, from Jacob to this blind man, their only credentials to spread the good news about God are that they encountered God. Their lives were transformed not by reading Scripture or hearing a life-

§ Pun intended – again.

changing sermon, but simply due to the fact their hearts were in a state able to be molded by the will of the Father.

Yes, for some, reading the Bible or hearing a powerful message might be the spark needed to make one's heart malleable to the transformative power of God, but it does not have to be.

Jacob's encounter with God happened in the midst of a competition. The Samaritan woman's encounter came simply doing a chore of her every day. The blind man's encounter occurred since he didn't let himself pity the situation he was born into. With all these varying situations, however, the same result occurred... lives were changed. Obviously the three main characters of these stories found their lives changed but look who else did because of them...

For Jacob, he set the example of how to be God fearing and worshipping as he impacted the lives of his brother and his own children. Eventually his obedience to the Lord would be nurtured into the creation of God's chosen nation. Furthermore, there would also be a well he dug which would be the site of another life-changing moment thousands of years later.

For the Samaritan woman at this well, her testimony saw an entire village come to understand the grace of God. And for the blind beggar, his story taught the Pharisees and Jesus's disciples an amazing lesson on spiritual blindness.

A second trait all these stories have in common is the transformation is not based on emotion but on action. Billy Graham once said, "Being a Christian is more than just an instantaneous conversion – it is a daily process whereby you grow to be more and more like Christ." We are saved from the consequence of hell in a moment, but our salvation is proved genuine over how we live out the rest of our days.

Usually Christian camps and conferences are notorious for playing on people's emotions and calling this result proof of transformation. If tears where the result of transformation, then Bambi, Old Yeller, and Up! are the best missionaries I know of.

In the stories above though, tears were not the common denominator, but action was. When we encounter Jesus, we seek to do His will and we desire to bring Him glory. This could mean forgiving someone who has wronged you in the past (or perhaps forgiving yourself) to boldly declaring your story and the Gospel to everyone who is willing to listen. Whatever the case, if transformation is not accompanied with action, then did anything really change?

Yes, it is true emotions in the moment could drive people to action and be the catalyst needed to begin the transformation of someone's life towards following Jesus daily. In this case however, I would argue emotion did not dictate the moment, rather the overwhelming presence of the Holy Spirit did. And since we are hard-pressed to understand the movement of the Spirit, we label its presence as something trivial like emotions.

A third and final thing bridging all these stories together is this – true transformation is not when we find God, but rather when God finds us. The story of the Gospel is not powerful because it tells of how we can find our way back to God, but it is powerful because it shows Jesus coming down to be with us – offering a way to bring us back to right standing with God. We are incapable of reconciling ourselves to God, but with Jesus we find hope and salvation.

If we truly desire to be transformed, either for the first time or for the thousandth, then perhaps the only step we need to take is surrendering control of our situation to God so He can do what only He can do.

Whether you seek transformation in your life or in the lives of others, why not begin with prayer asking our Lord to intervene in our hearts so that our lives may forever be different? Why not stop trying to find how we are defined in things of this world and start letting God give us longings for things of eternal worth? Why not let our life be molded to be more and more like that of Christ by letting His Spirit form us? Why not allow God to transform our name into a vessel He can use to point people to the Name above all Names?

So perhaps throughout this chapter, I have had my underlying message backwards... well let's fix that...

God encounters us → things change.

I'll conclude this chapter with one parting thought. While often this idea of transformation gets confused into only meaning the moment of initial salvation, I believe it entails much more. Transformation is not a one-time thing but rather it is a daily decision to allow your heart to be open to encountering God in a new way that day.

> *"Throw off your old sinful nature and your former way of life, which is corrupted by lust and deception. Instead, let the Spirit renew your thoughts and attitudes. Put on your new nature, created to be like God—truly righteous and holy."*
>
> *Ephesians 4:22-24*

And for the moments when life is tough, and the world is seeking to crush your transformation with thoughts of conformity, return to the basics. For just as a game like rock-paper-scissors revitalized can bring about a new sense of fun, returning to the childhood realization that "Jesus loves me this I know" and "God's got the whole world in His hands," might just be what it takes to remind you of how far God has brought you. Transformation doesn't have to occur through large prayers or divine revelations, but with simply declaring, "Jesus – you got this."

KELSEY'S STORY

While today I label myself as a God-fearing Christian, my life was not always like that. Through many obstacles during my life, my faith came into question several times. But when God showed up in my life through some new college friendships and to comfort me in tough times, I began to see my faith through a whole new lens.

When I was younger, my family all had a deep faith which was largely rooted my great-grandmother. My older brother and I grew up helping at the farm during the summer and fall with my great-grandparents. My brother would be out in the field with my grandpa and I would be in the house with my grandma cooking, baking, or cleaning to make sure everything was ready when the boys got back in.

My great-grandma each morning, had a routine when I would get to the farm. We would either start lunch for the boys (if it was something more than a sandwich and chips) or we would listen to church music while we ate. She would tell me stories about the songs, and we would sing and talk about the meaning. At this point of my life, at 5 years old I had nothing but faith in God largely thanks to my great-grandma.

Then the year 2006 hit. My life was flipped upside down. My great-grandma was diagnosed with cancer and passed away. If that wasn't enough, my grandma was diagnosed with cancer as well and passed away just a few weeks later. At this point, in my mind, my faith had passed away with them. It would be gone forever. For I questioned why this God that my great-grandma spoke so highly of would have taken away the two people that loved him with every piece of them.

Between that year and the beginning of high school, my faith was either nonexistent or very minimal. Then 2013 hit and again tragedy hit my family. My great-grandpa, who supported my whole softball career and was my best friend, passed away. And again, just a few months later, my grandpa then passed away. Any faith I might have had left was demolished.

Throughout the remainder of high school, I tried to build my faith and find new ways to find what I believed again. I went to church and went through the motions, but I was failing to find a solid foundation to build my faith upon.

Finally, college began. While for most college is a time of extremely difficulty, for me it was when I rediscovered faith in a whole new way. On my softball team, I had a teammate who I had heard talking about her faith and how she was trying to start a student ministry on campus alongside her dorky twin brother.* We began to talk and became friends. We would talk about our faith and I could slowly feel my foundation building again. When I thought all had been lost, God reached down and rescued me from my troubles.

Through friendship with my teammate, I realized my faith foundation would only stand strong when it was rooted in Jesus and Jesus alone – not my family, or a friend. Now, about to graduate, I find myself to have the strongest faith I have had in my life. And it was all thanks to God placing special people in my life to create a faith that I have always needed.

---

* Knowing the brother well, I do not think he would mind this description.

-Chapter 4-

A Story of Purpose

Imagine you are at your everyday job going through the motions just trying to make a living before a man you have never met yells at you from a distance to stop everything and come do what he wants you to do. You would be leaving the comfort and security of what you have known to go work for someone who has offered you no salary or pay or benefits whatsoever.

In fact, this new job, apart from getting to travel, will cause you much anxiety over the first few years working it. Not to mention will get you labeled as unfriendly to the local government and church. Now imagine you are crazy enough to actually decide to quit your current occupation to follow this man who yelled out at you. This basically is the story of Peter.

Matthew 4 tells the story of the temptation of Jesus in the wilderness, to Him beginning His earthly ministry, to calling the first of the disciples. In summary, this chapter finds Jesus walking away victorious from a direct confrontation with Satan to the start of the journey that would lead Him to ultimate victory over death. And in the midst of these monumental moments we see the Son of God go out of His way to reach out to an ordinary man named Peter:

> *While walking by the Sea of Galilee, he saw two brothers, Simon (who is called Peter) and Andrew his brother, casting a net into the sea, for they were fishermen. And he said to them, "**Follow me**, and I will make you fishers of men." Immediately they left their nets and followed him.*
>
> Matthew 4:18-20

Jesus did not have to start His relationship with Peter by breaking the ice or with meaningless small talk, but rather the first words He said to Peter were instruction guiding him to his ultimate purpose. Two simple words radically changed the direction of Peter's life – "follow me."

These words put Peter on a path where he would literally alter the course of world history through his obedience to Christ's command. He allowed Jesus to speak a divine purpose into his life before acting by abandoning his past and committing his all to what God had planned for his future.

This account of Peter beginning to walk with Christ holds huge implications on our faith journeys as well. Just as with Peter, we cannot truly begin to follow or know our purpose until we respond to Christ's call to follow him. Thankfully, we see Jesus say these exact words a couple dozen times throughout the four gospels and then this command is reemphasized throughout the remaining books of the New Testament – so clearly the invitation for each of us to follow is there. Notice however, while this command is a great stepping-stone towards realizing our ultimate purpose, as Peter would also soon learn, it is not the end goal.

Following in the footsteps of Jesus and devoting our lives to Him is part of our calling as Christians, but even this noble cause ends when we leave this earth. What then? We need a purpose that lasts as long as time itself – we need something to strive for that last an eternity. What this is ultimately is revealed through Jesus' worldly ministry.

As Jesus prays in John 17:3, *"And this is eternal life, that they know you the only true God."* And knowing God, knowing the Creator of the Universe, is accomplished through knowing the one He sent.

> *"I am the way, and the truth, and the life. No one comes to the Father except through me. If you had known me, you would have known my Father also. From now on you do know him and have seen him."*
>
> *John 14:6-7 (ESV)*

We fulfill eternity's purpose for our lives when we know the One who began all eternity. The way this is accomplished is through imitating Peter's actions by responding to the call to follow the Son. This is our ultimate purpose.

Is it really that simple? Could the chapter end here and you be satisfied with this knowledge you gained? My guess is no. I assume many of you understand our calling as Christians is to follow Christ, but the issue arises with the how. What does this command of "follow me" look like in our lives today and how can such a generic calling lead to unique journeys for each of us to walk? These are the questions I believe many Christians mean to ask when they say, "What is my purpose?" To find this answer, we must increase our understanding of what it means to follow.

Unfortunately, in today's technologically dependent culture we are cursed with a warped meaning of the word follow. To follow today often is associated with social media platforms like Instagram and Twitter.

If I follow someone, it means I could fall anywhere on a spectrum of complete obsession of a team or celebrity or I just simply clicked a button to add an individual as a friend based on an algorithm the app creators developed to suggest people I might know.

Whatever the case, to follow someone today does not mean we have to possess any personal connection with them. Following has created a social atmosphere where relationships are impersonal and built through virtual hearts and thumbs up.

What makes following people today appealing is the status it supposedly provides and the freedom to terminate who you follow without consequences. Neither of these luxuries come when we decide to follow Jesus. The word Jesus originally uses to call out to Peter literally is an interjection meaning 'to come now!' It is a command requiring action and submission.

As Peter's relationship with Jesus grew, the requirements behind the word follow grew as well. No longer did Jesus use the Greek word that meant merely 'to come' but instead began using the Greek word for follow meaning 'to join as one's disciple' and 'to accompany.'

For when Peter and the rest of the disciples followed, it was not merely a one-time click on a screen, but it was an ever-continuing responsibility to nurture the relationship they had with Jesus. To follow is to be obedient to the command of Christ.

Obedience in this case does not mean doing a lot of "Christian things" like attending church every week, buying your ticket to Passion a year in advance, or showing up 5 hours early to freeze your butt off standing in line for Winter Jam. Rather this obedience is equivalent to experiencing God in our everyday actions. And we experience God in our everyday when we succumb every day to God's plan. Let me warn you though, if you continue reading you will discover that we each have a plan and God has a plan. In order for life to work, one of these plans needs to be flexible and the other plan needs to be God's.

◊ ◊ ◊ ◊ ◊

Society today has trained us to pursue whatever our hearts and minds desire which at least in my life can be extremely dangerous because sometimes what I desire is very evil and definitely should not be pursued. That is why Romans 12:2, *"Don't copy the behavior and customs of this world, but let God transform you into a new person by changing the way you think. Then you will learn to know God's will for you, which is good and pleasing and perfect,"* is so counter-cultural today.

In order to follow God's plan, we must change our entire outlook. Why must we be transformed? Because if we were to piece together all Lord's commands into one sentence, innately we would find this plan is against our nature.

What would this one sentence look like? In my words: God's plan for our lives is *to live, to struggle, to ask questions,* and *to serve Him.*

The first part, "to live," seems elementary but as we read throughout Scripture, living does not mean surviving but prospering. God wants us to live a life of thriving not one of misery. Do not be deceived however! Prospering in life does not mean in terms of wealth, relationships, fame, or health like some preachers today might mislead you to believe. To prosper means to live in a manner pleasing to the Lord. It is living in a way where your actions seek to bring glory to the Father in the small and the large.

With this understanding the second part of the plan – "to struggle" – makes slightly more sense. 1 Peter 4:12-16 reads:

> *Dear friends, don't be surprised at the fiery trials you are going through, as if something strange were happening to you. Instead, be very glad – for these trials make you partners with Christ in his suffering, so that you will have the wonderful joy of seeing his glory when it is revealed to all the world. So be happy when you are insulted for being a Christian, for then the glorious Spirit of God rests upon you. If you suffer, however, it must not be for murder, stealing, making trouble, or prying into other people's affairs. But it is no shame to suffer for being a Christian. Praise God for the privilege of being called by his name!*

When we struggle, we are graced with the gift of experiencing just a taste of what Christ had to endure on our behalf. Yes, I know hearing part of God's purpose in our lives is that we would struggle is not ideal, but where would we be if we did not have to struggle?

If life was perfect and we never sinned, then there would be no need for a Savior. The fact struggling exists allows for the reality of a divine rescue to hold such an impactful weight. Also, our daily struggles allow us more chances to discover personally who God is and thirdly – "to ask questions."

God does not want us to have a blind faith. He did not create us to be robots only following His commands because we are programmed to do so but created us with choice. We have this crazy thing called free will because God knew in order for us to truly love Him, He could not force Himself upon us.

In fact, I think God appreciates it when we take time and wrestle with questions concerning our faith for it shows we seek growth. We just must be careful we do not reside in this state of wrestling for too long and exhaust ourselves. Sometimes we might be able to come to an answer but other times we must accept God ways are higher than our ways and move onto the most important part of God's plan for our lives – "to serve Him."

Serving ultimately means succumbing. Above I said we have free will, but when we decide to serve God, we choose to surrender our free will so God's will might work freely in our lives. When God's plan is the center of our existence, only then we start to know God like never before, thus our ultimate purpose begins to be completed. To follow Christ is to serve the Father like the Son did during His ministry so we might experience God. And experiencing God means becoming overwhelmed by His Spirit through our service.

Throughout the New Testament, we see Jesus and His disciples were often "filled with the Spirit of God" during their various journeys and encounters with others. However, as it becomes obvious in the book of Acts, one specific action undergone by the disciples led them to be "filled with the Spirit" more than any other... and no it was not during a "cry night" at a Christian camp. This act was *simple obedience* as Peter and the first disciples demonstrated in Matthew 4.

When a follower of Christ is obedient to the plan the Lord would have for him or her, they are overwhelmed by the Spirit. While specifics of this plan for each of us are difficult to discover, I can know one thing for certain – we are called to make disciples.

"Therefore, go and make disciples of all the nations, baptizing them in the name of the Father and the Son and the Holy Spirit. Teach these new disciples to obey all the commands I have given you. And be sure of this: I am with you always, even to the end of the age."

Matthew 28:19-20

We are told Christ will be with us always and I believe many of us want to believe that. Yet in life, when things get tough and we feel far from God, it is hard to convince oneself of this truth. But look at the context in which these verses were written... making disciples!

I know the Spirit works in mysterious ways and people definitely experience its power through nights of worship and the emotions of camps. However, what I also know is when the disciples were obedient to the Lord's plan and were seeking to make new disciples, they found themselves experiencing the overwhelming power of God. They took the message of the Gospel to the saint and the sinner, the Jew and the Gentile, the young and the old. And we too have this same responsibility.

To live, to struggle, to ask questions, to serve God – ultimately all these things are pieces in the disciple-making process. Our lives, the good and the ugly, the successes and the shortcomings, the obedience and the doubts, all are meant to provide us with a testimony of faith we can share with those around us.

For as I wrote above, our goal is to follow Christ in order to fulfill our purpose of knowing the Lord. Therefore, if we are to truly follow, we must have an active approach to sharing our story. To know God is to live in accordance to His plan for us which includes bringing glory to Him in all we do. What better way to bring Him glory than to make His Name known among all?

◊ ◊ ◊ ◊ ◊

Making disciples is great and all, but how exactly does this correlate to the unique calling God has for each of our lives? In 1 Corinthians 12 we read all of us are of one body but different parts clearly implying as members of the body of Christ we too are made with different responsibilities. Yes, ultimately all the parts of our body serve the greater purpose of keeping the body alive and functioning, but each system also is tasked with a specific purpose.

So far, this chapter has focused on the body as a whole in order to understand the importance of our general purpose. Now with the understanding of the general, we can move onto the specific...

Does God want me to become an overseas missionary? Am I to remain in a certain friend's life and witness to them or has the time come to move on? What job should I be in so that I can bring the most glory to God? Or once again in simple terms, "what is my purpose?"

While knowing God's general plan can be found by studying Scripture, knowing God's specific plan for each of our lives is much more difficult to grasp. Unfortunately, there is no step by step instruction manual from IKEA telling us how to piece together eternity's ultimate purpose into what our purpose in the moment consists of. Despite this however, we can take steps to see glimpses as to what God wants us to do in the present.

First and foremost, we must pray. Before Jesus was about to go to the cross to fulfill His purpose of conquering death, He found a secluded place in a garden to have a one on one conversation with God. He cried to the Lord asking if this was truly what the Lord had planned. For who better to ask of our purpose than the One who our purpose is meant to bring glory to?

Being honest however, many times these prayers of "Lord! What am I supposed to do!" find themselves unanswered – or at least we think they were unanswered. Most times in our lives, I believe God has placed quite visibly what it is we are to do right in front of us. We either ignore the signs or maybe we just do not know what to look for. Here is what I have found helpful: When seeking the specific, focus your gaze upon the intersection of these four things.

Your Ability.

Each of us have been given various gifts and talents we have the opportunity to use to glorify God. Some have been blessed with great speaking skills, some athletic prowess, some an incomprehensible ability to love, and still some wisdom beyond their age. Even the smallest and strangest of gifts, when nurtured correctly can be used to bring glory to the Father.

Your Affinity.

When one speaks of your affinity, they are referring to the things you are naturally passionate about. What things in your life are effortless to you because you enjoy the thing so much? Or to better understand this, look at the flipside of the issue – what things cause a holy discontent within you? Going through life, what problems do you see in society that cause you to want to take action? These are your affinities.

Other's Affirmation.
Unless you live completely isolated from all personal contact, then believe it or not other people will have opinions about your life. A healthy way to take in what other people are saying about you is to use their words to help discover your calling. Look at the tasks and skills where other people look to you for expertise or say you are naturally gifted at. Usually this is a good indicator of what abilities in your life will best be used to impact others.

Your Area of Opportunity.
We have been placed in this specific place at this specific time for a reason. God has placed various people and places for you to serve before you, you need only identify them. This could be using your workplace as your mission field or your teammates as people to witness too. Whatever the case, take hold of the opportunity you are in and make the most of it.

Discovering what lies in the intersection of these four criteria is a great stride towards stepping into the specific purpose God has for your life. For me, God has given me the ability and passion to write, often affirming it when I share my work with others. He has placed me on a college campus which was described to me as a graveyard for Christians when I was choosing my school. Furthermore, He has given me a desire to see the faith of my generation reignited. After prayer and self-reflection, it became clear this book was part of my purpose in this moment of my life. This book is at the intersection of the four above criteria.

Now how about you? Are you comfortable with where you stand in knowing your purpose or do you feel like there is

61

something more out there for you? Whatever the case, I implore you to take the time to explore the things in your intersection. Pursuing the intersection puts you at a great place to experience the full power of God at work. For when we are obedient to the plan of God, there is a sense of completeness and joy that will begin to overwhelm us.

As the disciples discovered in Acts and so also will you discover in your life if you choose to live for this great purpose – following God's plan is not easy. In Luke 9:23 Jesus instructs us, *"If anyone would come after me, let him deny himself and take up his cross daily and follow me."* Translated to today's lingo, following Jesus will not be a walk in the park. For if the world was against our Savior, we should expect the world to be against us as well.

This might be confusing because many people preach today when you are in God's will you are never safer. Unfortunately, this is a lie. Look at the apostles for example: Peter and Andrew were crucified, Paul was beheaded, James was clubbed to death, Thomas was pierced with spears, and Matthias was burnt alive. All great examples of men living out the purpose God had for them, yet not what I would describe as relative safety.

The truth of living for God is found in the bigger picture – when we are in God's will not even death should scare us or shake us from it. It is this radical obedience required of us to go all in to pursue our purpose.

Let's be real though, many times we might have the good intentions of complete devotion to the cause of Christ, but we just flat out fail. We find ourselves caught up in the temptations, busyness, trials, and pleasures of life we don't know what to do. Forget dying for our purpose if we cannot even live consistently for it.

As a basketball player, I think of standing at the free throw line about to shoot. My goal is to make it and I know

I have the ability to do so, but sometimes I am undisciplined and allow the fans behind the basket to distract me from my goal and I miss. A task I had trained for and have successfully completed many times in my career, I failed at in that instance.

Our life as Christians is similar to shooting free-throws. Our enemy is behind the basket trying to distract us from our purpose and sometimes they succeed. But God did not just give us one shot at the basket. He has given us as many as we need in order to make the shot. This is grace perfectly demonstrated. No matter how many failures, God remains with us standing at the line to help us make the shot He has called us to shoot.

Returning to Peter's story, we see even the man who Christ said He would build His Church upon would fail...

When Jesus was heading to the cross, Peter denied his Lord on three separate occasions and fled in cowardness after the crucifixion. At this moment, not only was Peter missing the basket, but he was shooting airballs. He was so unsure of himself and ashamed of his actions, he returned to a previous comfort of his – fishing.

After a time of unsuccessful fishing, Jesus appeared to Peter from the shore. The moment Peter recognized it was his Christ, he jumped from the boat to be with Jesus. They proceeded to eat breakfast together and have a mysterious déjà vu conversation in which Jesus redeemed Peter for his shortcomings. At the end of this dialogue, Jesus addresses Peter for one of the final times before ascending into Heaven. These words brought Peter's story full circle and renewed the divine mission in his life:

*And after saying this, He said to him, "**Follow me**."*

John 21:19

If you are lost in the craziness of life, return to Christ and let Him remind you what you are to do and most importantly who you are to do everything for. Take the command to follow and begin to live it out!

God does not just give purpose to your pastor's life but has given your life purpose and meaning as well. Recognize the general purpose through devotion to Scripture. Then spend time in reflection to find the specific purpose He has for you.

Find the things you are good at and have a passion for and nurture them into your divine calling. And when you get off track, return again to the simple command of "follow." Be obedient in the good moments and in the struggles, for in all moments there exists opportunities to make disciples. Share this amazing gift of grace you have been gifted so more and more may bring glory to the Father.

We should be overwhelmed with gratefulness of God's amazing favor towards us that we seek to serve Him in all we do. And when the time comes that God calls us home, we are not filled with sadness because we will lose everything we have amassed during our lives, but rather we will overflow with joy because we will get to enter a time of eternal praise of our Father. We do not fear death for death simply brings us the fulfillment of our purpose of knowing God.

So, I leave you with this question to think about next time you wonder "what is my purpose?" – instead ask, "Is my Jesus worth dying for?" Because if the answer is confidently yes, then truly living out your purpose by living for Him should be the simple next step.

EMILY'S STORY

Being in a tough academic program and trying to juggle all the other responsibilities of life has definitely had its ups and downs. I remember driving home from my pharmacy job one night, hurrying to get home so I could stay up late and study, while also needing to wake up at 4:30 AM for tennis practice... I get tired just thinking about it. On the drive home, I cried out to God, "What am I doing with my life? There has to be more than this." It was almost laughable how in over my head I felt. I was definitely "burnt out." It was like I was having a mid-life crisis, but then I quickly remembered that I was only 22.

What happened in that moment was I had forgotten my purpose. Understanding my purpose was not an easy, wisdom-in-a-flash kind of event. It took a lot of prayer and listening, and God continues to reveal what He's called me to do as I grow and experience new triumphs and trials.

A few years ago, I was gathered around a table with two older couples who have become my mentors. They have been such incredible examples for me of how to serve Christ and others well. One woman had lived in Russia for 10 years as a missionary and continues to oversee an organization there. During our dinner conversation, the question came up of how she decided to move and minister to that country. Her response was so simple yet profound, and it has really stuck with me.

In a time of prayer, she told God, "I'm available." That was it. The prayer wasn't extravagant. It wasn't said with an underlying agenda. She sincerely told God that she was ready for what He had in store. For her, it was moving to

65

Russia. For me, it was going to a college campus with a lot of brokenness.

When I started college and realized that being a Christian was a rarity, it was made clear to me how much I needed Christian community. Since there wasn't any on campus, I had to build it. By praying, "I'm available," God put me to the test and helped me to understand that my purpose was to serve right where He placed me. When He answered my prayer, I was not super happy with the response. I did not feel equipped to serve Him in that way; I was a quiet, behind-the-scenes kind of Christian. His purpose for me took me out of my comfort zone.

Engaging with college students first started as having a small Bible study and then going to get late night pancakes. Since then, He has led me and a few friends to create a St. Louis-wide college Christian ministry. God has called me to do things that I never would've done before. He has given me a voice and a boldness to share, and it all began by surrendering to Him the plans I had made for myself. I had to let go of control in order to find the One who has already orchestrated every detail of my life.

So, what is my purpose? To follow Him where He guides me and be willing to carry out whatever task He sets before me. As seasons change, He gives me new passions and opportunities, but He remains the same. He is always worth serving. Worth sharing. Worth living for.

-CHAPTER 5-

A STORY OF AUTHENTICITY

On the Saturday nights at college where I was not playing basketball or attending another sporting event, I often found myself participating in various board or card games with my friends. One such game (which is a personal favorite of mine) is a game called *Fakin' It*[*] – a game played through mobile devices and on the TV.

The idea of this game is each player is sent a set of instructions on their phones as to what to do. These actions could be anything from raising your hand if you have been out of the country to pointing at who in the room is most likely to not know the recipe for a grilled cheese.

Each round, all players are sent the same task apart from one unlucky individual who is sent "You are the Faker, do your best to blend in." After a few seconds, the TV counts down and everyone performs the task sent to them with the Faker trying to not attract attention to themselves. Then deliberation occurs (and friendships are tested) as everyone starts accusing everyone else of being the Faker. A vote then happens and if the Faker can survive three rounds of tasks

---

[*] One of the games included in The Jackbox Party Pack 3.

without ever having the group agree unanimously that they are the Faker, then they win. Needless to say, winning as Faker is difficult.

There was one time in particular I was playing this game and my friend Kevin (who I chose not to kill a few chapters ago) and I had to share a phone since at the time he still owned a flip phone. At first, we did not see an issue with being on the same team because we would just follow the prompt sent to my phone and react honestly... this proved difficult though when we were assigned the role of Faker.

After two rounds of quietly sitting in the corner, the group we were playing with had pretty much eliminated all other possibilities of who the Faker was leaving all suspicion on us. Round three would prove to be vital – we survive, Kevin and I win... if not, the Faker loses like usual. Prompts are sent out and the countdown began.

3...2...1...

Kevin raises his hand and I keep my hand down. Yikes! This is the first time we did not do the same action – we are totally caught. Yet the room was filled with noiseless confusion. The other players were convinced from this we could not be the Faker! For the prompt sent out was this: "If you are blonde, raise your hand." Care to guess between me and Kevin, who is blonde and who is not?

The vote happens and Kevin and I escape as Faker, thus winning the game! I'd say it was our deceptive skill which won it, but obviously luck had a part to play. Unfortunately, this luck would run out, because the very next game which we were selected to be Faker again, Kevin and I were caught round 1. We could fake it for a while, but eventually we were exposed for the frauds the game made us out to be.

Can you see a possible tie in with the titled theme of this chapter? How many people who call themselves Christians could be revealed to be nothing more than just playing the role of Faker in this game called life?

We are called to live our lives with authenticity, and as I stated when writing about integrity, we are not to wear a mask. Our walks with Christ should not be just trying to fit in with the crowd nor trying to deceive others into thinking we are something we are not. Rather they should be grounded in a genuine desire to grow closer to the Lord we serve. Christian is not merely a label we fill in on a form, but a lifestyle we have been called to.

This journey we find ourselves on is not a game where we can cheat our way through. With *Fakin' It,* you can implement various strategies to help you trick your opponents – with the simplest being merely copying the actions of other players. This will not work when it comes to faith!

One cannot begin a relationship with God by relying on the actions of another person. It is not as simple as repeating a prayer after a pastor or coming forward during an altar call... salvation is not found through following the actions of man but allowing the Son of Man to act for you.

Whatever you do, do not confuse this calling as a passive role. Passivity in our walks with Christ will ultimately result in the same thing as passivity in the game – eventually we will be called to act, and unless we know what we are to do, we will be discovered as a faker. James 2:14-18, 26 (ESV) reads,

> *What good is it, my brothers, if someone says he has faith but does not have works? Can that faith save him? If a brother or sister is poorly clothed and lacking in daily food, and one of you says to them, "Go in peace, be warmed and filled," without giving them the things needed for*

the body, what good is that? So also faith by itself, if it does not have works, is dead.

But someone will say, "You have faith and I have works." Show me your faith apart from your works, and I will show you my faith by my works... For as the body apart from the spirit is dead, so also faith apart from works is dead.

The mark of an authentic believer is one which acts upon the great purpose they have been given. They do not have to fake being Christian by attending church on Sunday and posting Philippians 4:13 as their Instagram profile description, because their love, joy, and service is all the evidence needed to prove their faith.

Sure, you can survive faking a walk with Christ all you want. You might even fool your friends and family and perhaps even yourself for a while. But where does that leave you at the end of the day? Either you are all in or there is no point at all.

Where are you at? Are you living a life on mission dedicating yourself to a life of prayer, sacrifice, and Christian fellowship? Or are you a Christian because your family is? Are you living in hypocrisy trying to get the benefits of faith all the while enjoying the pleasures this world is offering you? Is God going to look at you and recognize you are the Faker within the group, or will He smile upon you as you are truthfully fulfilling the purpose He has for your life?

◊ ◊ ◊ ◊ ◊

If Jesus was on Twitter today or if He pastored a modern-day megachurch, I am convinced His popularity would not be all that impressive. In fact, I would venture to say even those who say they would follow Him would end up unfollowing Him soon after. His church services would not be televised because TV stations would not tolerate low ratings. And I bet His social media profile would never be on the featured page. Yet, none of this would bother Christ at all. In fact, He would probably have expected these exact results.

During Jesus' ministry on Earth, He never concerned Himself with the quantity of His following but with the genuineness of those who did follow. He never sugarcoated what He needed to say in order to attract more people. He never spent millions on elaborate marketing campaigns to announce the cities He would be visiting. Jesus knew the cost of following Him was high and He knew many people would not be willing to pay such a cost. This fact is demonstrated greatly in the story of the rich young ruler.

> As Jesus was starting out on his way to Jerusalem, a man came running up to him, knelt down, and asked, "Good Teacher, what must I do to inherit eternal life?"
>
> "Why do you call me good?" Jesus asked. "Only God is truly good. But to answer your question, you know the commandments: 'You must not murder. You must not commit adultery. You must not steal. You must not testify falsely. You must not cheat anyone. Honor your father and mother.'"
>
> "Teacher," the man replied, "I've obeyed all these commandments since I was young."
>
> Looking at the man, Jesus felt genuine love for him. "There is still one thing you haven't done," he told him. "Go and sell all your possessions

and give the money to the poor, and you will
have treasure in heaven. Then come, follow me."
At this the man's face fell, and he went away
sad, for he had many possessions.

Mark 10:17-22

The beginning of this story should be the dream scenario for any Christian seeking to make disciples. Absolutely no effort was needed because the young man approached willingly and sought a relationship with Jesus without having to be coerced or guilted into it. If I was Jesus in this account, my first thought would have been "Heaven just increased size by one!" Obviously though, I am not Jesus, and this was not what happened.

Jesus did not allow Himself to water down His message at the opportunity to lead this ruler into a relationship with Him. For Christ knew the motives of the man's heart. With this account, we as disciples of Christ are revealed two categories of individuals to be cautious about on our journey – two types of inauthentic Christians.

The first of these types I refer to as the "Heaven as an Insurance Policy" Christian. In the story above, we see the rich man begin his conversation with Jesus by asking what it is he must do to have eternal life. In other words, how does he get into heaven? If we are viewing our spiritual walks like this, we are missing the point of Christianity altogether. We are wrongly mistaking our goal of faith with the final destination of our faithfulness.

Romans 10:9 states, "*If you confess with your mouth that Jesus is Lord and believe in your heart that God raised him from the dead, you will be saved*" (ESV). When we truly begin walking with Christ, our future is secure. Our place in Heaven is being prepared for us and there is nothing more we need to do to "get into Heaven."

As we see in Ephesians 2, our salvation is a gift we have been given through grace and our faith. If it required more of us, then I would have a hard time seeing how Heaven could be called a gift.

And if receiving this gift was the goal of Christianity, then everything we will ever do on our Christian journey could be counted as worthless. This is why the goal of faith should not be and has never been merely punching a ticket to Heaven for the sake of eternal life. Our goal, or as last chapter says – our purpose, is to know God. Authenticity is about a relationship, not about the reward we receive.

Now do not hear me wrong – this is not me downplaying the greatness of Heaven, but rather challenging our misconceptions concerning it. The "Insurance Policy" Christians are dangerous for they demean Heaven to simply someplace we go when we die... it is a "get out of jail free" card concerning hell.

On the other hand, an authentic follower sees Heaven as the destination where our relationship with God becomes its most intimate... for in Heaven we are rejoined with our Father in perfect union. Authentic Christians look towards the day they are called home to Heaven while maintaining an attitude of genuine commitment to Christ now.

For God did not save us so we would not end up in hell; He saved us so we could shake the very gates of hell! Truly devoting our lives to Christ means going to battle daily for Him. And if our battle for our faith leads to the end of our time here on Earth, then we can take comfort in knowing our place in Heaven has been secured for us by our Savior.

The second type of "Christian" to be weary of hinted at in Mark 10 is the "Light Show Concert" Christian. This type of inauthentic believer has all the right traits and is ready to do something amazing, but at the end of the day their motives behind their beliefs are wrongly placed. With the young man, he was so attached to following the rules and to the possession of riches he was unable to bring himself to follow Jesus.

We can follow all the rules and do all the "Christian things" we are supposed to do, but at the end of the day are we willing to sacrifice ourselves? Can we let the lights of our own stage be redirected to point towards our Heavenly Father or will we covet the fame and glory for ourselves? Past this, will we be satisfied if our walks with Christ come without any of the luxuries we have come to expect living in this country?

Take the modern-day American church for example – get rid of all the lights and sounds and the fancy prop infested sermons, and would you still be satisfied with just Jesus? Unfortunately, many Christians today would not be. We have come to Christ and continue to follow Him because it is a tasteful and entertaining experience. We have no problem spending hundreds of dollars for front row tickets to our favorite Christian concert, but we hesitate to give money to the homeless, sick, and needy.

Christ has called out to us to be prepared to give up our everything in order to follow Him. Yet we have become so attached to the comforts of life that our desires begin to be more for the creation than the Creator. The only songs that should be playing during our life's concert as a true believer are "Christ Alone" and "Christ is Enough." A fancy production is not needed for us to live out our faith but simple reliance on Jesus is.

◊ ◊ ◊ ◊ ◊

There are people out there, perhaps you reading this right now, who are truly living for the present and not merely striving for Heaven. They are more than willing to sacrifice everything if the call to do so ever comes. Yet the struggle with authenticity continues.

Do not hear me wrong, every single follower of Christ will have to battle with hypocrisy, and it will feel like this conflict is never ending. I also know though we are not called to a state of complacency... we are not to become stagnant. Therefore, we must continue to fight for our faith by combating what might hold us back from becoming more Christ-like. And for many of us this means facing a major fear of ours.

As humans we have an innate desire to fit in with the crowd around us. We want people to like us and accept us therefore we block off a key lesson about authenticity. Jesus demonstrated we should not get caught up in the "number of Facebook friends" we have, but rather stick to the truth of the Gospel. Quality over quantity. This is where many of us are tripped up however in our pursuit of authentic faith. We struggle because we fear rejection.

What happens if my friends don't accept the radical lifestyle I would be adopting by following Christ? How am I supposed to reach the lost if no one will listen to me? What if people say no?

The fear of being rejected is one of the greatest fears people face in society today. Because of this fear, we find ourselves living safe lives. We only act if we know our actions will be perceived well. We only fulfill our purpose when it is easy to do. We only proclaim the name of Jesus when we won't be judged for doing so. Maybe Scripture says this is how we are to approach life and our fears and my Bible just happens to be missing that part, but I doubt that to be the case...

Paul addresses our fears of living out our faith when He writes 2 Timothy 1:7-8:

For God has not given us a spirit of fear and timidity, but of power, love, and self-discipline. So never be ashamed to tell others about our Lord. And don't be ashamed of me, either, even though I'm in prison for him. With the strength God gives you, be ready to suffer with me for the sake of the Good News.

For Paul, suffering meant being thrown in prison, and for us it might mean we are rejected by those closest to us. But with the power that dwells in us, we are able to boldly proclaim our story and the Good News! Yes, the possibility of rejection will always exist. However, thinking deeply about this issue, no matter what life you live, rejection will remain a possible outcome.

We might be rejected here on Earth, but is that not better than the alternative of finding ourselves rejected when we stand before the Father in Heaven? For me, I believe three of the scariest verses in Scripture come during Jesus's Sermon on the Mount. And if the importance of authenticity has not been seen throughout this chapter, these verses are sure to change that:

"Not everyone who says to me, 'Lord, Lord,' will enter the kingdom of heaven, but the one who does the will of my Father who is in heaven. On that day many will say to me, 'Lord, Lord, did we not prophesy in your name, and cast out demons in your name, and do many mighty works in your name?' And then will I declare to them, 'I never knew you; depart from me, you workers of lawlessness.'"

Matthew 7:21-23 (NIV)

In plain English, Jesus is saying one day to the people who have faked their way through Christianity He will tell them to get away. This is the ultimate rejection and I know I do not want to be on the negative end of that statement.

So, the question then arises, do you want to be rejected by man or by God? The answer you find here will ultimately guide you to the path you will walk.

Choose to walk with Christ and there might be times you face rejection, yet this will not faze you since you know you have found decisive acceptance in God's eyes. Choose the other path and face possible rejection still on Earth and definite rejection when the decision of your eternal residency is up for verdict. I pray each of you choose the most logical of these options.

Therefore, if we are to devote our lives to authenticity, what exactly does it look like? Obviously, authentic Christians are those rooted in prayer, love, and sacrifice (no it is not a coincidence these are the topics of the next chapters), and true believers are living out their divine purpose, but what more? Simply put, authenticity is discovered when we are simultaneously pursuing vulnerability.

Another translation of 2 Timothy 1:8 says, *"Do not be ashamed of the testimony about our Lord..."* (ESV) meaning we should have a sense of confidence when telling the story of Christ at work in our lives. We need to tell of the good, bad, and ugly of our lives so that we might be able to connect with those around us. All of us need redemption and renewal – there is no point in hiding it!

Be vulnerable with those you are trying to take the Gospel to and expect to be surprised! For in honesty, we allow for others the opportunity to connect with the story God has given us. Through our trials as well as our victories, we are able to relate to various people and hear them say "me too." And what are the significance of these words? In their simplicity, when someone says "me too", they are declaring they understand where you have been meaning they can see hope to arrive at the same place you are now.

Vulnerability then is not an invitation to look down on the failures of others nor is it the time to glorify the shortcomings in our lives, but rather introduce light into dark situations. Through telling our story and reaching out in relation to those God has placed in our lives, we protect ourselves from pride and begin fulfilling our purpose.

> *I don't mean to say that I have already achieved these things or that I have already reached perfection. But I press on to possess that perfection for which Christ Jesus first possessed me. No, dear brothers and sisters, I have not achieved it, but I focus on this one thing: Forgetting the past and looking forward to what lies ahead, I press on to reach the end of the race and receive the heavenly prize for which God, through Christ Jesus, is calling us.*
>
> *Philippians 3:12-14*

Perhaps up until this point in your walk with Christ, authentic would not be a word you use to describe your faith. If that is the case, then you took a step towards authenticity without knowing it. Because through honest self-evaluation, or being vulnerable with ourselves, we will all come to realize this trait is one that is not easily obtained. Many moments in life, we will feel as if we are just playing the role of Faker, but we must discipline ourselves not to stay in this mindset.

Learn from the mistakes of the past and allow them to be the rising action pointing to the climax of your future. Run this race God has set before you by remaining faithful through the dirty sections of life and remember it is the Lord that has called you to this journey and it is relying on Him that will get you through to the end.

Just imagine if every Christian reading this truly lived the life they have been called to live. Imagine if the millions of Christians who said they believed were authentic in their belief how the world would change. God willing, I hope that happens, but in the meantime let us each begin in our own lives.

Let us be faithful with what we have been given and let us be bold in our purpose so maybe we can fulfill the cliché of "one person can change the world." Jesus did it while He lived as a man; why not allow Him to do it again through working in our lives?

MARK'S STORY

I had just reported back to campus for summer school following my first year of college. I walked into my head coach's office for a quick catch up. I remember him telling me how he had just gotten back from a special medical procedure in Kentucky. You see, Coach Kennedy of Texas A&M had been diagnosed a few years earlier with Parkinson's disease. Parkinson's is a disorder of the central nervous system that affects movement and often is accompanied with a lot of tremors. To put it plainly, it was unprecedented that Coach Kennedy was still leading a high-major basketball program during a fight with Parkinson's.

But I was extremely thankful he was still coaching for he taught me much. For he is an extremely faithful man and ran his program like a ministry in many regards. And it was he who has given me insight to what it means to live with authenticity. So, let me tell you about the most authentic person I've ever met in the basketball world...

Nearly every single day my team began our work in the film room with a devotion or Scripture reading. We never rushed it and there was always a higher-purpose lesson to gain. Sure, my coach loved basketball and had won at a very high level... but this... this is what he cared about the most. Whether it was after a big win or during a dreadful losing streak, we never failed to have a team devotion or Scripture reading to start the day. Especially when we were on a losing streak or going through hard times, Coach Kennedy put even more of an emphasis on turning to the Lord.

81

For my coach's instinct during his own personal fight with Parkinson's was to lean into his faith so it was only natural for my team to take after him in tough times and do the same. And I think it was that instinct to turn to God in rough times (and also in good times) that truly shows someone's authenticity level. My coach had a consistent inclination to hand the keys over to God and that's what made me realize how genuine and authentic he was. That is what made me seek to be authentic in my life.

We will never be completely "authentic" during our time here on earth. True and complete authenticity will only come when we arrive in Heaven. But I do believe we see glimpses of it in our own lives. Authenticity shines through in tough times and remains during the good. You see the heart and intentions of people in all moments. I'm just lucky to have seen an authentic leader and authentic believer take all the challenges and hardships of college basketball and his own life and point it back to God. After all, we are most *authentic* when we are emulating Jesus... when we have the humility and learned-instinct to submit to God and turn to Him in every circumstance.

But in order for authenticity for truly show itself in our lives, we must decide to trust God 24/7. We must put our faith in God no matter what we are facing. Let us stop fronting and surrender our all to God.

-CHAPTER 6-

A STORY OF PRAYER

Recently I have been thinking on the question "What is the greatest lesson I have ever been taught?" As I am at the end of my undergraduate journey in college, this question is allowing me to reflect upon all the courses I have taken at my time at Millikin University as well as evaluate what I held onto from the countless hours of study and class discussion.

Instantly, many ideas come to mind as to the greatest lesson: my Eastern Philosophy class where we often practiced the art of meditation, my Gendered Communication class where I became more familiar with the reasoning of individuals who I might disagree on issues with, my Abstract Algebra class which showed me how to take complex problems and simplify them down into workable pieces. In short, my educational experience has been fulfilling and enlightening.

Yet, when I take a moment to truly think of the greatest lesson college has taught me, I cannot help but conclude this lesson was not found while sitting in a desk listening to old men and women with doctorates. Rather it came sitting in a pew at an FCA weekend camp. And the teacher was a man in his sophomore year of high school...

I have had the privilege to lead many high school students while serving as a counselor at FCA camps. Whether this be at a guy's weekend retreat to a high school huddle leadership conference, many of my most fond memories in college have come while helping mentor those just a few years my minor.

One of these moments that I hold most dear came during leading a guy's camp in St. Louis in which a young man (let's call him Chad) poured out his heart before me during the final night of camp.

Throughout the weekend, Chad had been relatively reserved during all of our group discussions. Aside from the fact he played baseball and attended a high school I knew of, my knowledge of who he was extremely thin. This changed drastically the final night of camp.

As I have stated in previous chapters, and many of you probably know if you have experienced Christians camps, the final night can be filled with remarkable life-changing decisions. Yes, it is filled with emotional highs, but just as often can one find signs of true transformation – as was the case with Chad.

The night began to wind down and I sat alone in the back of the chapel allowing the guys in my group to have their space to make whatever decision they needed to make. For Chad, this decision meant coming to open up to me about his life.

From an external perspective, you might assume Chad's life was pretty good. He had a great personality, was extremely blessed athletically, and was able to form friendships with ease. But that night the external would do no good in hiding the chaos he constantly fought internally. In an unscripted moment of vulnerability, Chad revealed to me his struggles with various temptations in romantic relationships, an issue with his health he was constantly battling, and described to me one of the most shocking home environments I had ever heard of.

Without saying too much on the specifics, I can say if I was in Chad's shoes, I would not have been able to put on a happy face as well and as long as he had done in his life. I wanted so bad to just be able to take away some of the burden he felt. At this time though, all I could do was sit and listen.

After a while, when he finished speaking, I did the one thing I believed would help him the most – I prayed. A less mature spiritual me would have attempted to provide him with advice of how to make his situation better and perhaps if his situation was simpler I would have done so that night. However, the complexity of the storm Chad faced and the fact I myself had little control over my emotional response after listening, God revealed to me prayer was the only option.

What we prayed about I cannot remember. But I do know eventually the camp director came and tapped me on the shoulder telling me it was time to wrap things up. Little did either Chad or I realize, but we had spent close to two hours talking and praying, meaning the chapel had cleared out by the time we finished. So, we said our "amens" and departed to our rooms to go to bed.

Camp ended the next day, with Chad and I parting ways – he back to high school and I back to college. Over the next few months, I would often text him to see how life was going and to my disbelief, his home situation changed little to none despite my constant prayers on his behalf.

Up until this point in my life, I knew when praying there would always be a possibility God would not respond in the way I wanted Him to; but in this instance, I felt as if God was not responding at all. Matthew 21:22 declares if we ask something in prayer and remain faithful, we will receive. This was not occurring in my mind. However, I would soon learn I could not have been more mistaken.

Fast forward more months and many prayers later, Chad and I found ourselves together again this time at a co-ed FCA leadership camp. While I was excited to see him back at an FCA camp, I knew talking to him would be difficult especially after how much I knew of his life. The first few days of camp, we both went about our own business for he was not in my group this time around. A few times our paths would cross as we competed in various activities, but we never had an opportunity to truly catch up on life – that is until the final night came.

Once again, the message this night was laced with a sense of urgency and emotions flooded the room as the worship band repeated the chorus of *Good, Good Father* over and over. As per usual during this moment as a leader, I retreated to my place in the back. I was quickly pursued by Chad. He approached me with a smile on his face and before I could say a word, he embraced me with a large hug. What followed from here, could only be described as an act of God.

Chad told me how he appreciated my prayer I said over him at the last camp for it radically changed his life over the months following camp. Then he paused and said to me two words which I consider to be the greatest lesson anyone has ever taught me. What were these words? Simply – "Prayer works."

While at first, I found myself confused by his declaration since I knew how little things had changed in his life this past year, but his explanation left me speechless. He realized far better than I that all the prayers we said might have done little to change his circumstance, but they were monumental in changing his perspective. I was hoping God would change the situation, but Chad was rejoicing of the fact God was transforming his heart.

All the trials he had to go through and continued to face were making Chad realize how to rely on the strength of the Lord rather than trust in his own abilities. Furthermore, these storms he had to go through made him appreciate Christ's sacrifice on the cross even more.

We as sinful men and women deserve the evil in our lives. For by nature we are evil since it is written all have sinned and fallen short of the glory of God (Romans 3:23). Chad saw not only did he deserve everything bad happening to him, but he deserved death. Yet through Christ – a man deserving of no evil for He had committed none – our slates are wiped clean. Jesus conquered death so we could have life. To Chad, if that meant living life having to fight everything the enemy has put against him so he can know God, then it is worth it.

What is even crazier, in the weeks following leaving this leadership camp I received a couple texts from Chad telling me of how vastly improved his home life was. To him this was unexpected, but to me I believe this was just God showing off saying not only could He change someone's heart, but He could do the simpler task of fixing someone's external issues as well.

Wow did this encounter hit me hard. Sure, I had the knowledge prayer can be the catalyst needed for a miracle and can radically transform lives, but until this conversation with Chad, I did not fully believe in it.

So how about you? Do you believe in the power of prayer? Or are you like I was and might just do it on occasion because it is the "Christian" thing to do? Whatever the case might be, I pray the rest of this chapter will lead you to recognize the power and purpose of prayer like Chad did. I pray for your prayers to be able to shift situations from disastrous to remarkable, but above all I pray each and every individual reading this finds their heart transformed by prayer.

I will do my best to lay out a handful of things the Bible says about prayer in the words to follow, but in order to completely grasp this cornerstone of our faith, you must allow God to reveal it to you. How does this happen? You pray.

◊   ◊   ◊   ◊   ◊

Jesus is without question the most influential man to ever walk on this Earth. Whether you believe in Him as a Messiah or not, it is impossible to denounce His existence as a man. And as a man, Jesus spent much of His time teaching those around Him various lessons on how to handle money, how to treat your wife and kids, and even how to fish. He was a teacher with many fields of expertise for He was also God who knew all.

Twelve men were blessed with the opportunity to follow Christ during His three-year ministry on Earth and during this time they learned all about life from the greatest teacher ever. They did not have to ask to be taught, for the heart of Jesus was to teach His followers through all things. However, on one particular occasion, the Disciples broke routine and ended up asking to be taught on a specific topic. Luke 11:1 provides us this story:

> Once Jesus was in a certain place praying. As he finished, one of his disciples came to him and said, "Lord, teach us to pray..."

Out of all things the Disciples could have asked the Lord Jesus to teach them, they asked about how to pray. This alone should indicate the importance and necessity of prayer to us.

Before arriving at the how to pray, I believe it to be wise to first look at the when and where questions about prayer. For if we are unable to overcome questions of when and where, forget trying to arrive at the how. Why? Because we will not even be praying in order for the how to even matter. To accomplish this, let us use the prayer life of Jesus as our guide.

Question 1: When did Jesus pray?

Throughout the four Gospels, the authors recorded numerous times in which Jesus prayed. He prayed at His baptism (Luke 3:21-22), after He miraculously fed 5000 (Matt. 14:22-23), after an exhausting night of ministry (Mark 32-35), before choosing the 12 Apostles (Luke 12-13), and before He went to the cross (Matt. 26:36-44) just to name a few.

Jesus found the proper time to pray was during big life moments, after great victories, when He got home from a busy day, before making major life decisions, and while fulfilling God's purpose for His life. Basically, to Christ, the proper time to pray was always.

He would begin His day with prayer, end His day with prayer, and fill His day with prayer. In short, if Jesus felt as if something in His life would be better handled in the hands of His Father, then He would pray about it. And you guessed it, Christ knew everything was better off in His Father's hands.

To Jesus, prayer was not an item to be checked off on spiritual checklist, but it was as instinctual and necessary as breathing. 1 Thessalonians 5:16-18 (ESV) reads:

*Rejoice always, **pray without ceasing**, give thanks in all circumstances; for this is the will of God in Christ Jesus for you.*

As followers of Christ, we should be in constant communication with our Lord and Maker. We pray without ceasing for we know of the power of the One who sits at the other end of our prayers. When we have worries, we pray (Philippians 4:6a). When we are in trouble, we pray (James 5:13). When we are thankful, we pray (Ephesians 1:16). In all things, we pray!

Sometimes though it feels as if we get too busy in order to have time for prayer. Our culture requires us to have our foot on the gas 24/7. This means prayer often will find itself in the backseat. This should not be the case. Martin Luther once wrote, "I have so much to do that I shall spend the first three hours of my day in prayer." He realized the only way he would accomplish anything of any importance would require the action of God. For if we are too busy to take things in our lives to God, then we are flat out too busy.

Question 2: Where did Jesus pray?

From what you just read about the when, you might be able to guess the answer to the where would be similar. To an extent, you would be right. Jesus did not let a location prohibit His prayers. He would pray wherever He found Himself during His journey. But if we dissect a handful of locations of His prayers mentioned in the Bible, a trend begins to emerge.

Jesus prayed in a secluded place (Mark 1:35), in the wilderness (Luke 5:16), on a mountain (Matt. 14:23, Luke 6:12), in the Garden of Gethsemane (Matt. 26:36), and to put it most clearly, Jesus prayed alone (Luke 9:18). Christ viewed spending time alone with God and away from the troubles of this world as essential.

We should not be surprised in Matthew 6:6, Jesus instructed His disciples to go into their closets, close the door, and pray in secret. For prayer is not a public spectacular announcing our holiness to the world but is a private event where we speak with God.

You might find it difficult to completely isolate yourself from this world (which I would then argue you are not trying hard enough), but even then, it is possible to be alone in the middle of a crowd. If your mind focuses on the One you are talking to and blocks out all the external distractions,* I do not see why fulfilling prayer cannot happen while surrounded by many other people. For prayer is not about what position your body is in, but what condition your heart is in.

Are you praying with faith according to God's will? Are you praying with devotion and thanksgiving? Are you praying in the Holy Spirit? If so, it does not matter where you find yourself for you are alone with God.

One might ask however where praying with other people and in group settings come in to play? I mean the Bible does instruct us to pray for one another so we might find healing (James 5:16), and I do not dispute this at all. But even then, we can do so as an individual in private to our Father in Heaven. Prayer was never meant to be a public undertaking but reserved for when we are alone with God.

Is it wrong to pray in public and with others then? No, I do not believe this to be the case. Christ warns us about public prayer because of the wrong intentions public prayer could be said under. When we are with others, our prayers could be twisted into trying to say what they want to hear.

---

* Including the big distraction that often resides in many of our pockets.

91

This is what Christ calls as hypocritical... it might as well not be prayer at all.

But when we return to making our prayer between us and God, and not solely for the benefit of anyone who might be listening, then I believe we are really just practicing praying alone while surrounded by a crowd.

Now we have a better understanding of the when and where, let us return to the question the Disciples asked Jesus.

Question 3: How did Jesus pray?

The answer Jesus gave in Luke 11 was what we called the Lord's Prayer, which can also be found in more complete detail in Matthew 6:9-13 (NIV).

> *"Our Father in heaven, hallowed be your name. Your kingdom come, your will be done, on earth as it is in heaven. Give us this day our daily bread, and forgive us our debts, as we also have forgiven our debtors. And lead us not into temptation, but deliver us from the evil one."*

A simple way to understand the components of this prayer is through a clever acrostic guide. The way Jesus taught His disciples to pray, and essentially us, can be simplified into ACTS.

A – Adoration. This component of prayer is the most important yet is often the one we skip over the easiest. Adoration is spending time to glorify the Father for who He is. In the Lord's prayer, adoration is implied in the petition "hallowed be your name." We are taking time in prayer to take notice of God's amazing attributes and praising Him for them. If you do not know where to begin, reading the book of Psalms is a great place to start for adorations are all over the place there. If you want a few suggestions try Psalm 8, 19, 29, 33, 47, 65, 93, 95, 111, 139, and 150 (just to list a few).

C – Confession. We make mistakes, but thankfully we serve God who provides us limitless grace and mercy. If we confess our sins to the Lord, He is faithful to forgive and cleanse us from all unrighteousness (1 John 1:9). Yes, this is difficult for we must expose the parts of ourselves we probably are not proud of, but remember God already knows about all our sin. When we confess, we are doing more than merely stating what we did wrong, but we are joining in agreement with God in recognizing our sin. And recognizing an issue is a great first step in overcoming it. Just as in the Lord's Prayer, we must pray "forgive us our debts."

T – Thanksgiving. While adoration is adoring God for who He is, thanksgiving is praising Him for all He has done and provided. We have been given so much, therefore let us show thanks! And in the moments of life where finding something to be thankful for might be difficult, remember we can never seize proclaiming our gratefulness for Christ's sacrifice on the cross.

S – Supplication. Many times, when we pray, our prayers might take the form of SSSS over ACTS. We have no issue treating God like a genie providing Him a Christmas list of our wants and desires. Yes, supplication (or asking for God's provision) is a key component of prayer but it should not be the sole component. God wants us to ask Him for things for He loves providing, but when we ask, it should remain for the glorification of the Lord. Not only should we pray "give us this day our daily bread," but we should recognize and are thankful for the fact God will meet our needs. We tell Him what we need and thank Him for all He has done (Philippians 4:6b).

If you are just beginning the journey towards a more vibrant prayer life, remaining true to the structure of this acrostic is a great place to start. Take notice though! This is a starting point and not the end. As we grow in spiritual maturity, so also can we grow in prayer. All the components of ACTS remain, but we have personalized it in order to best communicate with our Father. And is not communication with God what prayer is all about?

Do not let yourself trying to stick to this formula distract you for the purpose of the act you are participating in. Prayer, above all, is a conversation with God. Just as we seek to converse with people in our lives we have relationships with, so also should we seek God in conversation.

We talk to Him because we are interested in hearing what He has to say. We talk to Him so we can express our appreciation of everything He has done. We talk to Him since we desire to grow closer to Him. We talk to Him because we love Him.

For the moments we do not know what to say or perhaps are too broken to articulate our thoughts into words, we have the Holy Spirit in us interceding on our behalf. Romans 8:26 (ESV) declares:

> *"The Spirit helps us in our weakness. For we do not know what to pray for as we ought, but the Spirit himself intercedes for us with groanings too deep for words."*

In our moments of struggle, the moaning from our soul is music to our Messiah. He wants to help us in life, therefore even when we can't bring ourselves to Him in prayer, He is already acting on our behalf. For prayer is occurring even when we are unfaithful to pray.

If you have ever tried to have a conversation with just yourself, you might know it is difficult to do and likely you will be labeled strange for talking to yourself. Sometimes though it could be easy to feel prayer is like this... it is of course just us talking to Someone who does not talk back, right? Think again.

God has said more during His part of the conversation than we can ever say through our prayers. As prayer is us speaking to the Lord, the Bible is the Lord speaking to us – why else would it be called the Word of God? 2 Timothy 3:16 tells us all Scripture is *"breathed out by God"* allowing us to know His responses to our prayers. Therefore, when we are looking for answers, let us dive into Scripture.

Reading and studying the Bible allow us to align our thoughts, actions, and words towards the Will of the Lord. Our prayers no longer are us talking to the blankness of our wall and ceiling for we are hearing God's voice. Because when we become more familiar with His Word it is inevitable we will also become more familiar with His voice.

There is a reason I rely so heavily on Scripture throughout all my chapters and it is because I know God speaks to us through it. And having God speak to you through this book is of much higher value than listening to what I have to say. Once again this is why I will encourage you to look deeper into the passages I have included and take time to read them in the Bible yourself. For having God's word in your heart is greater than having a Bible on your bookshelf.

Reading our Bible and devoting ourselves to prayer is more than an obligation of Christianity but are foundational to our faith. Through these disciplines, we learn more about God and learn more about ourselves. Life requires much from us, but through prayer and knowing God's Word, we can find a new perspective and power to approach life with.

Like my friend Chad found, when we devote ourselves to prayer and are faithful to believe God is working on our behalf, the struggles of this life will be overcome easier and the victories are all the greater.

I realize there is much about prayer we will not understand nor did I touch on in this chapter, but let us not let the ignorance of this rob us from the blessing and privilege of prayer's use. Knowing all the theology behind prayer has its benefits but getting to know God more through actual application of prayer is infinitely better.

DREW'S STORY

Going into college I didn't expect to be challenged so much trying to balance life as a student and life as a baseball player. I found myself surrounded by players that I watched on TV in high school while attending classes surrounded by twenty thousand other students. I felt lost. So unknowingly, I searched for an identity that would allow me to fit in. But the person I was becoming was one that did not have Christ at the forefront of their life.

I did not realize that until a day during my baseball season freshman year when one of our team captains and an assistant coach approached me saying I had not seemed focused on the field. They called me in for a meeting with just the two of them. As a freshman I didn't really know what to think. I was intimidated by these two guys but at the same time grateful that they cared enough about me to call me in and talk.

The topic of this discussion was developing a routine for myself on and off the field. They went on to tell me that routines are a way to stay consistent and during times of struggle they allow us to relocate our minds to refocus onto the topic at hand. I immediately felt intrigued. I never once thought about routines being things to fall back on when life goes off the rails.

They asked me "what is something you can do to regain focus in any moment on or off the field?" At first, I didn't have the slightest idea of what I could use, so the captain told me his methods. He went on to say that his routines involved music in the morning and before games to get his mind in the place it needed to be in to compete in the classroom and on the ball field. He said that his music sculpted him into the person he is day by day. It is his identity.

After that meeting I immediately called my parents and after a long talk on the phone I realized what I needed was something that I have been doing since I was a little kid – prayer. Prayer was to be a vital part of my identity. Like that captain who used his identity to fuel his drive throughout the day, I used mine. I needed those precious moments spent with Christ in every aspect of my day.

I realized that whenever I am in times of distress or need, prayer is my answer. From that point forward I made prayer my routine. And this decision came at the perfect time for my life was about to become even more crazy. I was blessed to find myself on a team that came up just one game short of the College World Series and then I also found myself drafted by the Oakland Athletics of the MLB. Prayer and communication with my Father was what helped me navigate that time. To this day, prayer remains an important part of my life from when I wake up to every time I step foot in the batter's box.

Our routines make us who we are, they identify us. In college and in life, inconsistency causes us to lack identity. While routines allow us to stay relatively consistent. However, there is no way for our routines to be unwavering and for us to remain faithful without Christ being the source. And personally, I can't think of better routine to develop than that of talking with the God who defines my identity in the first place. For I am a son, brother, grandson, and a baseball player but above all I am a child of the one true King.

-CHAPTER 7-

A STORY OF LOVE

We have all heard the sayings "it is love at first sight" and "I am falling in love." Hollywood spends millions of dollars per year to convince us our true love exists. If only we wait (and get extremely lucky it seems), we too can have the picture-perfect ending of riding off into the sunset with our soulmate. Our "other half" is out there, we just have to be courageous enough to begin looking.

While these beliefs make for some great movies, I am not convinced this is how love truly operates in real life. Many times, I witness those closest to me "fall in love" with their "true love" only to find themselves breaking up after the honey-moon phase of the relationship ends. Words are exchanged which probably were best left unsaid, and groups of friends are forced to choose sides. Yet, in most cases, a month passes and both parties have already moved onto the next relationship. Seems to me, the previous declaration of true love might have been premature.

What happens next? If society has anything to say on the matter, this pattern of "falling in love" will continue until people just settle for a mediocre relationship. I mean, why else would divorce rates be so high?* What else are we to expect? When I think of "falling" into something, it is my experience someone usually gets hurt... why would love not be subject to the same fate?

When we fall into love, the implication arises that falling out of love becomes possible. This contradicts everything I know about what love actually is. So perhaps, these phrases and thoughts about love our society has adopted need to be reworked. Instead of referring to love, maybe what Hollywood is trying to teach us is how to be enticed by attraction. Is this not the goal of love as our culture has defined?

Love today is largely romantic and is discovered through the stigma of sexualization. There is a reason the pornographic industry makes more money per year than the NFL, Netflix, and Disney bring in individually.† People crave images of love and will often resort to wild fantasies to satisfy their desires. Maybe it might not be through pornography, but through the thousands of romantic movies found through the dozens of video-streaming services.

Whatever the case, to me it appears many are finding it difficult to love because love has lost its meaning. People today are compromising their definition of love to that of false notions the entertainment industry feeds us all.

Why is this the case? Because we all yearn for love... to be loved and to be able to love. We settle for lower standards of love for we fear going through life unloved. Even Oxford defines love to be "an intense feeling of deep affection," and as a verb "feeling a deep romantic or sexual attraction to someone." These twisted definitions of love should not

---

* The American Psychological Association reports 40 to 50 percent of married couples in the United States divorce.
† Per Yahoo Finance, Harvard Cyber Research, and other sources.

satisfy us! We long for something deeper and from what I can tell, letting society define this amazing thing of love is the wrong course of action.

If we want to know love, we must stop letting everyone around us define it first. We must find refuge in knowing our God has already made clear to us what love is. To discover the truth, we must disconnect from our preconceived ideas and rely on God to take us back to the origin of this concept.

There exists a vast amount of wisdom we can discover about this spectacular four-letter word, and it would be impossible for me to even come close to writing about it all in this short chapter. Even authors who have devoted entire books on the concept of love have only skimmed the surface of everything there is to know. This why I will only look at a few specific aspects of love in the words that follow.

But while I might not be able to fully express every detail about love, I do know this – we do not increase in our ability to love based upon gathering more information about it, but by practicing it. Love is not meant to just be something we learn about only to store in the back of our brain. It is meant to be lived out in our everyday lives.

As I wrote about in the chapter about purpose, our purpose is to know God and to live according to His plan… we do this by knowing love and living in love. For as 1 John 4:8 declares: "God is love."

◊ ◊ ◊ ◊ ◊

Even if you have never been to church before, odds are you know of the Ten Commandments. You might not know exactly what all ten are, but you have an idea of why they exist. Supposedly, following these Ten Commandments will help us to live moral and good lives. Non-Christians will even agree many of the Ten Commandments are necessary for society to survive...thou shalt not murder, thou shalt not steal, thou shalt not lie, just to name a few.

But of all ten, and all the other rules we find throughout Scripture, what command is the most important? Jesus tells us the answer in Matthew 22:36-40:

> *"Teacher, which is the most important commandment in the law of Moses?"*
>
> *Jesus replied, "'You must love the Lord your God with all your heart, all your soul, and all your mind.' This is the first and greatest commandment. A second is equally important: 'Love your neighbor as yourself.' The entire law and all the demands of the prophets are based on these two commandments."*

As a Christian, love is not optional, *love is a command!* And not only is it a command, it is the most important one! For through love, all the other commands in Scripture are fulfilled.

We do not worship idols, for we love God. We do not use the name of the Lord in vain, for we love God. We do not kill, steal, covet, lie, or commit adultery, for we love others. All our actions spawn from the notion of love.

If you are like me however, you take serious issue with Jesus's answer in Matthew 22. He was asked for the most important command and He listed two separate things. What is greater? Loving God or loving others?

To answer this, consider this question – what side of the penny is more valuable, heads or tails? The answer of course is both. Without one side, the other side is worthless. Heads needs tails and vice versa. The same holds true with these Great Commandments. Jesus's answer is two sides of the same coin. Our love for God is expressed through how we love His Creation. And we cannot begin to love people without first realizing love comes from God.

We love God with all our hearts, souls, and mind when we are loving others as we love ourselves. This means loving those who are easy to love, but also loving those who deserve anything but love. For the mark of authentic love is found in how you treat those who society say is okay to hate.

Just before Jesus was crucified, He demonstrated this type of love. With the knowledge that Judas had set off to betray Him and with Peter just days away from denying Him three times, Christ said to His disciples, *"Just as I have loved you, you should love each other. Your love for one another will prove to the world that you are my disciples"* (John 13:34-35). Jesus was able to say this to people He knew would be turning on Him. He did not say love others based upon how they will love you back, but simply commanded all of us to love others like He did. Period.

An excellent example of how Christ loved others is found in the story of Barabbas (found in Matthew 27). Per Jewish custom, one criminal on death row would be released during the Passover celebration and in this instance, the Roman Governor allowed the crowds to choose. Would it be Barabbas – a murderer, enemy of the state, and leader of an insurrection, or Jesus – a man even Pilate couldn't find guilty of any crime? Low and behold, the crowd selected Barabbas.

What did Jesus do? Did He rise up in protest? Did He begin to preach how unfair this system was? No. He accepted His fate for He knew fulfilling His purpose would allow people deserving of punishment to receive grace and mercy. In order to show God's love for the world by sacrificing Himself on the cross, Christ first had to love

Barabbas. The pieces of wood meant for a murderer would now be used to kill our Savior.

How did Barabbas respond to this amazing gift? No one knows for certain, but I would venture to say it is safe to assume he never turned to Jesus and proclaimed his thankfulness. The first person to benefit from Jesus taking up the cross, never once showed any appreciation or remorse. Odds are Barabbas went back to being Barabbas.

I believe Christ knew this. Jesus knew in order for love to be complete, He had to love those who would never love Him in return. He had to love those who would openly mock, betray, and deny Him. He had to love the unlovable. And this love Jesus commands of us, demonstrates we truly are His disciples.

Today, this would be considered countercultural. Even the best of us usually will not go around loving our enemies and loving those who disagree with us. Sure, we might tolerate them, but loving them is a different issue entirely. Hear me clearly though – to tolerate someone does not mean you love them! In fact, I would warn against toleration at all.

Looking at the book of Revelation reveals to us a lesson on this trait of tolerance. One of the seven cities in Revelation, Thyatira is the least known and least impressive, yet the author of Revelation had the most to say to them. The church of Ephesus was praised for its good deeds and Thyatira was even better for it also had the love for all that Ephesus lacked (see Rev. 2). Where was Thyatira's flaw? It was in her tolerance.

The church let itself be corrupted by the sins of a member and refused to part ways with the sinful nature. The "love" the church showed was ultimately undiscerning and blindly affirming for tolerance had overcome it. Tolerance is not love; it is unfaithfulness.

We must pursue the love Jesus preached and embodied. Risky, radical, costly, inconvenient love. Messy, complicated, demanding love. Love of neighbor, stranger, and enemy.

Jesus loved the sinner and was intolerant toward the evil that enslaved the sinner. To the adulteress He said, "*Neither do I condemn you; go and sin no more*" (John 8:11, ESV). He forgave her because He loved her; but He condemned her sin because He loathed it with a holy hatred.

This is how we should be. We should not be tolerant of the sin of society around us. Tolerance costs us nothing, but loving others will require us to sacrifice much. Our schedules will be interrupted when we love others. Relationships might be lost because we value someone's eternal residency over letting them continue to live enslaved to sin.

Does this intolerance mean the people we love might deny our love? Yes, for there will always exist a Barabbas in our lives; but this does not change what we have been called to do.

Recognize we owe no one anything expect for the obligation to love them (Romans 13:8). And the greatest love we can show them is pointing them towards Jesus and living in a manner consistent to the way the Lord has instructed us to live. This is why the Great Commission in Matthew 28 goes hand and hand with the Great Commandment in Matthew 22. It is our love for others that urges us to share the Good News with them. And it is persevering in faithfulness through this command so that others might one day step into this strange sensation of love we offer through Christ's demonstration and power.

Love is a command, because through love we fulfill our purpose. We cannot love others until we love God, and we cannot not love God until we learn to obey Him. Thus, to love begins with obeying the commands the Lord has given us.

◊ ◊ ◊ ◊ ◊

A second theme of love found throughout Scripture is the idea *love is unconditional*. To me, this concept is difficult to grasp because human mentality dictates we should not cross oceans for people who would not cross a puddle for us. We attach conditions onto how it is we should love and ultimately how we should live.

These conditions manifest themselves in our lives in a variety of ways. We have to perform in school, if we are to be successful. We have to be cool, if other people are to like us. We have to meet unrealistic standards, if we are to be considered to have any worth. If we work hard, if we don't quit, if we ___, then life will be better.

Because these conditional statements are so relevant and apparent in our lives, it makes sense we have attached these same conditional sentiments onto traits like love. When we do this however, we mistake the type of love God commands of us in Scripture. Worse yet – we mistake the type of love God has for us.

With the mindset above, it is logically consistent to conclude God will only love us if we read our Bible, if we go to church, if we pray, if we play nice, and if we never once sin. If we do all the right things and if we avoid doing any of the wrong things, then God will love us. While this is the way the world works, this is not how our God operates!

The two-letter word we should be focusing on is not "if" but rather "so." God loves us so we seek to know Him better through prayer, church, and reading Scripture. God loves us so we do not have to worry about where our worth is defined. God loves us so we now have a choice to follow His direction for our lives.

Unconditional love is not waiting for the other party to act first, but it is taking the initiative into its own hands risking that it will not be reciprocated. And the greatest news ever is God offers this love to all of us! He loves us all so He Himself set off on a rescue mission 2000 years ago to save us from the penalty of our sin. This is what unconditional love is.

A great way this type of love is demonstrated is through the well-known parable of the Prodigal Son found in Luke 15:12-24.

> *A man had two sons. The younger son told his father, "I want my share of your estate now before you die." So his father agreed to divide his wealth between his sons.*

> *A few days later this younger son packed all his belongings and moved to a distant land, and there he wasted all his money in wild living. About the time his money ran out, a great famine swept over the land, and he began to starve. He persuaded a local farmer to hire him, and the man sent him into his fields to feed the pigs. The young man became so hungry that even the pods he was feeding the pigs looked good to him. But no one gave him anything.*

> *When he finally came to his senses, he said to himself, "At home even the hired servants have food enough to spare, and here I am dying of hunger... so he returned home to his father. And while he was still a long way off, his father saw him coming. Filled with love and compassion, he ran to his son, embraced him, and kissed him.*

His son said to him, "Father, I have sinned against both heaven and you, and I am no longer worthy of being called your son."

"But his father said to the servants, "Quick! Bring the finest robe in the house and put it on him. Get a ring for his finger and sandals for his feet. And kill the calf we have been fattening. We must celebrate with a feast, for this son of mine was dead and has now returned to life. He was lost, but now he is found." So the party began.

So the party began... a son who squandered his inheritance on wild living ultimately returns home to an entirely new type of celebration. No longer did the youngest son have to indulge himself with what this world had to offer, for his father had offered him an alternative option. His father offered to his son what our Father offers to us – an invitation to experience love.

What is special about this type of love is that it allows for us to decide not to love God back. In the story of the Prodigal Son, the father loved and supported his son so much he willing gave his youngest son his portion of the family wealth, despite how culturally insulting this request was. The father gave his son room to make reckless decisions and do with whatever he wanted with his freedom. And when a famine swept over the land and there became a shortage of food, there was never a shortage of love.

Eventually the youngest son would return and instead of holding a grudge or making his son work off his debt, the father ran with open arms and embraced his son. Why? Because he was his son and he was home. A son who had rejected his father's love had been brought so low in order to realize when all else had gone, love still remained. In a decision that can only be described as humiliating, the son accepted the invitation to experience his father's love.

This is our story as well. No matter what we have done, God is ready on the starting blocks waiting to run and welcome us home. He is loving us now, even if we are dismissing Him. He is waiting for us to pull the trigger releasing His love into our lives to fully embrace us.

No matter how many times you have gotten completely wasted on the weekend can change how much God loves you. No matter how many times you have succumbed to laziness, lying, pride, or lust can change how much God loves you.

No matter how many mission trips you have been on can change God's love for you. No matter how much you have given to charities can change God's love for you. No matter how much you share His Name can change God's love for you. No matter what you do can change how much God loves you!

This is what unconditional love is all about and this is what makes our Lord so great. Because if God's love for me was based on what I did, then I would not be in good shape even given the amount of "good" I think I have done.

We can never truly understand God and His love, but we can show our appreciation for it through our daily lives. When we live in accordance to the Spirit, we have the ability to love flowing through us and all of the sudden our actions change. No longer are we bound by a desire to sin but rather a longing to honor God in all we do and glorify His name. And once again this is not of our own doing but because we have Christ in us.

Our society has twisted the concept of love beyond recognition. But when God reveals Himself to us and we allow Him to guide our path, we go from relying on our understanding of love to allowing God's unconditional love to resonate through us. We become a means God uses to demonstrate His love to those who have yet to enter into a genuine relationship with Him. Prodigal sons and daughters exist all around us, why don't we be the storytellers of the Father's love to them?

◊ ◊ ◊ ◊ ◊

This leads to the third and final theme of love I will discuss in this chapter. Put simply it is this: *Love requires action.*

The story of the Prodigal Son demonstrates the act of unconditional love through the action of the father running to his lost son. The story of God's unconditional love for us is shown through the action of God creating us, letting us live free to choose our own direction in life, and ultimately one day coming again to save us from all the evils of this world (among an infinite list of other things).‡ But how about us? What actions can we take in order to truly demonstrate this trait of love.

If you ask anybody who has been around the church for a while "what is one passage which discusses what love is best?" you will get a variety of answers. But one reoccurring response will be what has become known as the love chapter, aka 1 Corinthians 13. And to me, I believe I would be doing a disservice if I did not discuss (though only briefly) this passage within this chapter.

> *Love is patient and kind. Love is not jealous or boastful or proud or rude. It does not demand its own way. It is not irritable, and it keeps no record of being wronged. It does not rejoice about*

---

‡ Honestly, take a moment here to think of all the ways God has shown His love for you. Write a few of them down somewhere and when life gets tough pull out this list as a reminder of how God's love has gotten you this far and how it will continue to carry you in this time of need.

injustice but rejoices whenever the truth wins out. Love never gives up, never loses faith, is always hopeful, and endures through every circumstance.

Prophecy and speaking in unknown languages and special knowledge will become useless. But love will last forever!

1 Corinthians 13:4-8

Is the emphasis of this passage on feelings or actions? Hopefully you can see the latter of the two is the correct answer. For when we are living a life of love, we are men and women of patience, kindness, humility, forgiveness, faithfulness, hope, and perseverance.

Our culture will do its best to convince us the actions of love cease at the end of bed covers. Once again, let us not let our understanding of love be so shallow.

Let us have the confidence and boldness to declare we are going to love others no matter what. Just as Romans 8 tells us neither death nor life nor the powers of hell can separate us from God's love, so also should we pursue the same love for others. And let us not just merely say we love each other with our words, let us show our love to be true and genuine by our actions (1 John 3:18).

Putting the three themes in this chapter together leaves us with this command: Act with unconditional love. Love those who might turn their back on you and who might never love you back, like Jesus loved Judas, Peter, and Barabbas. Love those who have insulted you and seek reconciliation, like the Father loved the prodigal son. In short, love people like God loves you.

Will this be possible? If the responsibility rest solely on us, no it is not. But when we tap into the Divine source of love, we can begin loving like never before. We no longer are

111

"falling into love" for we are living in love. The God of the Universe, the God who is ultimately love itself, lives and acts through us. We are not burdened with the task of loving others, because God's perfect love is covering us.

In all our actions, the love described in 1 Corinthians 13 radiates through us because we have become convinced how God defines love is better than any substitute a popular movie can provide.

Love is not a temporary pleasure meant to fulfill us in a moment of sexual desire, but is a continuous action meant to fulfill us in all moments, from before our birth to after our death. Love never ends.

And when life becomes too much to handle, and it seems as if love has been overcome by evil, try to recall the greatest act of love ever undergone in human history. You won't find it on movie marathons hosted by the Hallmark Channel, and you won't find it surfing through the darkness of the Internet.

You will find it hanging on two planks of wood wearing a crown of thorns. For the greatest act of love in history, and how we are to fulfill the command of love bestowed upon us, begins and ends with the understanding and implementation of one wonderful word... one absolutely amazing action. Love is achieved at its highest level through sacrifice...

PAUL'S STORY

For me, it seems that my whole being has infinitely improved as I've put myself aside and *loved* others without thought of gain or repercussion. While this lesson has been revealed in many ways to me, there is one story that showed me that the power of Jesus-style love should not be underestimated.

I have the privilege of serving as a leader in the Fellowship of Christian Athletes on my campus. My college has such an awesome congregation and having this sweet, sweet gathering in the middle of the week is so refreshing and encouraging. We never turn a person away, athlete or not, and that brings forth many wonderful relationships and plenty of interesting characters. One such character was named Clark. Clark was a transfer student who came from an interesting home life and had previously wrestled at a community college. To me, he was a guy who would cross any line and possessed many challenging traits.

As one can imagine, when somebody comes into the group and creeps out the girls, disrespects leadership, and pulls from the productivity of the discussion, it is incredibly hard to even accept them – much less love them!

While many of the members at FCA were able to accept him, I was not seeing much *love*. Everyone put up with him (to his face) but wanted nothing to do with him or his soul. And that is where I felt God convict me. God was calling me to be intentional, vulnerable, and give Clark something truly special – my time.

Within a few weeks, he called me one of his best friends. But honestly, he encompassed every single pet peeve and character trait that pushed my buttons, so I can't say I felt the same so quickly. Yet, I kept hanging out with him despite how badly I wanted to do literally anything else but hear his pessimism, slander, and disrespect. Four days a week, my phone would whistle, "hey, wanna go shoot?" and Clark and I would go play 1-on-1 basketball for hours without end.

Reflecting on my time with him, I truly think no one ever tried to actually form a true friendship with him. People danced around conversations with him, telling him what he wanted to hear, trying to keep his fuse from blowing (and it was short). But our relationship was built on vulnerability, boldness, discussion, and *love*. It may be hard to believe, but through spending time *loving* him as an overflow from my love for Jesus, he began to help me grow. It was Proverbs 27:17 in full effect. Clark had equipped me to love other difficult people and showed me what *love* is capable of when you put yourself and the opinions of others aside.

After months of people telling me to leave him behind and stop burdening myself with his problems, I got to see his heart change drastically. I was so thankful that I had stuck with him and pointed him to the cross so many times (despite how mad my persistence might have made him). His empathy, compassion, and patience grew more than I could have imagined. At the end of the day, the *love* I had for Clark became genuine and effortless. And now I am blessed to be able to call him one of my best friends.

-CHAPTER 8-

A STORY OF SACRIFICE

As I sit here writing this chapter, we are only a few weeks away from the highly anticipated squeal of Disney's 2013 animated phenomenon. Yes, I am of course referring to *Frozen 2*. For months after the original's release, the country was obsessed with Elsa, Anna, and Olaf. Disney fans could not get over the shocking success of this instant classic. You could say in terms of this film, millions of Americans could not Let it Go.*

For me, I was fangirling over the genius of this movie for a while. From great sing-along tunes to the fact this was not a sequel or remake of a pre-existing film, this tale from Arendelle quickly became one of my favorites. Approximately after the dozenth time I watched this movie, I discovered something from it which solidified a spot for *Frozen* in my list of top ten go to movies. This lesson sets this movie apart from almost every other film currently being made and it is this lesson we must take to heart if we are to call ourselves followers of Christ. That all said, let me now set the scene for you (Careful! Spoilers ahead) ...

---

* Sorry about that pun... Couldn't keep it in, heaven knows I've tried.

The movie focuses around two sisters, Anna and Elsa, and their journey from playful children to eventual leaders of their kingdom. When they were young, they would often enjoy one another's company by using Elsa's magic power of controlling ice and snow to create a world of fun and games. One day however, Elsa accidently injured her sister Anna with her powers leading the King and Queen to take both of their daughters to a colony of trolls in order to heal Anna.

These trolls saved Anna while offering a warning to Elsa about the consequences that would arise if she failed to learn to control her powers. This warning created a situation where both sisters were left isolated within the castle and ultimately formed a rift in the relationship between Elsa and Anna. Elsa shut Anna out leading to both sisters to struggle with insecurities.

Years later when Elsa became old enough to become crowned as queen of Arendelle (due to both her parents being killed by a violent storm while at sea), fear consumed her. She was terrified of what would become of her if the kingdom discovered her powers or what would happen if she hurt Anna once again. Alas, Elsa lost control after her coronation and the build-up of years of not using her powers led her to engulf the kingdom in an everlasting winter. She fled to the mountains after realizing what she had done.

Fast-forward a bit and we see Anna venture out to save her kingdom from the winter and more importantly save her sister from herself. After leaving a man, Hans, she had just "fallen in love with" in charge, Anna traveled out on foot to find Elsa. On the journey she met an ice-harvester named Kristoff and a talking snowman named Olaf. Together this group of misfits traveled to the ice palace Elsa had created.

Anna confronted Elsa and in a series of unfortunate events, Elsa accidently froze Anna's heart.

Anna, Kristoff, and Olaf left the palace to return to Arendelle, but Anna fell more and more ill as they journeyed back. After coming across the colony of trolls that originally saved Anna as a child on their journey, they discovered only an act of true love could save Anna. The group raced home so Hans could kiss Anna and save her.

Now if this was any other Disney movie, the prince would kiss the princess and happily ever after would flash on screen. Role credits, right? But the climax and conclusion are what set *Frozen* apart from all other Disney princess films...

Anna learned Hans was never interested in love but only in power, so he betrayed the princess by locking her in a room thus sealing her fate of becoming a princess popsicle. During this time Elsa returned to the scene only for Hans to lie to her that her actions had killed her sister. Visibly distraught, Elsa fell to her knees crying allowing Hans to use the cover of a blizzard to kill her and complete his plan to secure control of the kingdom. But Olaf broke Anna out of the room she was locked in at just the right moment for Anna to throw herself between the sword of Hans and her sister. This self-sacrifice ultimately constituted itself as the act of true love needed to save Anna.

Through this scene and the remainder of the film, the two sisters realized love was the only way to control the power Elsa had been given and above all they discovered what true love is.

True love is not found in a kiss, but in the act of sacrifice. Our culture will do its best to cover up this truth by feeding us images of love being defined by one-night stands and outward appearance, but every now and then even

Hollywood realizes the truth about this amazing thing called love.

I believe the reason *Frozen* found so much success was because movie-watchers became dissatisfied with the empty promises of the typical portrayal of love and were welcoming of the genuineness of love portrayed in this film. They were able to connect with it at a personal level because this story of sacrifice has been written on all our hearts.

Whether you identify as a Christian or not, we all have been shown and told a story of a love that mimics that which was depicted in *Frozen*. But this particular story of love is not confined to a cinematic screen but rather is revealed to us in every blade of grass, drop of rain, and grain of sand. The love for us is so great, not even the concept of infinity can compete with the vastness of what I speak of...

> *You see, at just the right time, when we were still powerless, Christ died for the ungodly. Very rarely will anyone die for a righteous person, though for a good person someone might possibly dare to die. But God demonstrates his own love for us in this: While we were still sinners, Christ died for us.*
>
> Romans 5:6-8 (NIV)

Our God's love for us is demonstrated in the truth He died for us even when we are not living for Him. Jesus sacrificed His comfort in Heaven and sacrificed His life on Earth for us so we could know the Father. Without this sacrifice, there is no salvation... there exists no purpose... we have no hope.

Like Elsa, without sacrifice we would only be left wandering in the wilderness, struggling to find relationships, and ultimately on our knees waiting for the sword to come down and end it all. But with the intercession of a sacrificial action, we can rise from our grief and lostness and discover that we were given great power to be kings and queens! We of course are the sons and daughters of the Kings of Kings!

When we accept the greatness of the sacrifice made on our behalf, we find new confidence to lead a life of joy. Just as Anna and Elsa opened the gates of Arendelle so every traveler could share in the magic found within their kingdom, so also has God opened the gates of Heaven allowing us to point people towards the entrance so we can all share in the marvels found of the greatest Kingdom ever!

What is the best way to point people towards this Kingdom? It is by demonstrating the same type of love and sacrifice to others as God demonstrated to us. When we lay down our lives for the cause of Christ, our lives become a movie used to show others a sneak peek of the truth of Romans 5.

Therefore, when we take after the example of Christ and choose to sacrifice, we introduce purpose into a world which is wandering around aimlessly. We provide hope to people seeking something greater in life. We love those who have never experienced this amazing freedom. This all begins with the decision to sacrifice.

◊ ◊ ◊ ◊ ◊

One of the greatest books I have ever read is *Not a Fan* by Christian author and pastor Kyle Idleman. In this book, Kyle discusses what it means to become a completely committed follower of Christ. Honestly, for anyone wanting to be further challenged in their faith, this is a must read. While the entire book is great, one topic he writes on sticks out to me still to this day and relates extremely well to the ideas to be expressed in this chapter.

When thinking on the topic of sacrifice, Kyle concludes that sacrifice as a Christian ultimately means answering the call to follow Christ. And from there, to fully follow Christ means making the conscious decision to go all in for Him. For God has called us to a purpose-filled life and now it is our responsibility to answer the call to follow Jesus – to wherever, at whenever, with whatever. This is sacrifice.

A passage Kyle uses to demonstrate this point, which I will also discuss, is Luke 9:57-62. In this story, Luke gives us the record of Jesus's encounter with three men each of which had a different restraint holding them back from following Jesus fully.

> As they were walking along, someone said to Jesus, "I will follow you wherever you go." But Jesus replied, "Foxes have dens to live in, and birds have nests, but the Son of Man has no place even to lay his head."
>
> He said to another person, "Come, follow me." The man agreed, but he said, "Lord, first let me return home and bury my father." But Jesus told him, "Let the spiritually dead bury their own dead! Your duty is to go and preach about the Kingdom of God."
>
> Another said, "Yes, Lord, I will follow you, but first let me say good-bye to my family." But Jesus told him, "Anyone who puts a hand to the plow and then looks back is not fit for the Kingdom of God."

Wherever, whenever, whatever. These are the requirements of us if we are to choose to sacrifice our all for the sake of the Gospel.

In the first encounter, Jesus admits to the man the reality of following Him could mean homelessness... it could cost us our comfort. *Wherever* means following Jesus on Sunday mornings in church, but past that it means following Jesus in places we are not comfortable doing so or perhaps not even safe.

This is contradictory to many messages being preached in the American church today. We are told coming to Christ means living a life of prosperity and comfort, which is true just not in the way we imagine it.

We prosper because we recognize our treasure is stored for us in Heaven and we are comforted in knowing the Holy Spirit resides in us to help us through the trials of life. Yet, we seek more.

As the great theologian C.S. Lewis puts it so eloquently, "It is quite useless knocking at the door of heaven for earthly comfort. It's not the sort of comfort they supply there." Sacrificing for Jesus means realizing our personal comfort might have to be pushed to the back burner. For many, this will be tough to do, but this does not change the fact we have still been called to do it.

This might cause a funny feeling inside you at first, but to quote another great author of the last century, Dr. Seuss, "from there to here, and here to there, funny things are everywhere."† And just as funny things are everywhere, so also is Christ calling us to follow.

To some, this might mean answering a call to travel overseas, while to others it might mean answering the equally difficult calling of following Jesus in your home, at your school, and on your team. Whatever the case is, do not

---

† From Dr. Seuss' *One Fish, Two Fish, Red Fish, Blue Fish.*

make like the first man in Luke 9 and fail to sacrifice your comfort in order to follow Christ. By doing this, you also might find a type of comfort you never knew existed.

"For the more we suffer for Christ, the more God will shower us with his comfort through Christ."
2 Corinthians 1:5

An equally important lesson is the directive to follow Jesus *whenever* He calls us. Are we willing to sacrifice our commitments and possibly even some relationships in order to take up our cross after Jesus? Or are we just waiting for a more proper time to do so? Because I tell you what – there is no time like right now to decide to become fully devoted to Jesus.

No one is guaranteed tomorrow; therefore, we must decide today is the moment we will sacrifice all. Yes, the cost here is high and as the second man in Luke 9 discovered, it might even require missing the funeral of a loved one.

This might cause you to think, why is Jesus so inconsiderate of the needs of this man that he can't even attend his father's burial? And by asking that, we would be missing the point.

Doing what Jesus asks of us means we sacrifice our convenience. Will He ask us to skip our parents' funeral to follow Him? It is doubtful. But if He did, are you willing? This is the question we must answer when faced with following Jesus whenever. It is a question of commitment and above all it is a question of urgency (but more on that in chapter 10).

Finally, we have been called to be ready to sacrifice *whatever* to follow Christ. As stated above, this could be comfort, safety, relationships, and convenience, but sacrifice could also cost us our time, money, and esteem. Under normal circumstances, no one would ever do this, but with the love and passion of Christ flowing through our veins, these actions don't just become possible, but we recognize why they are worth it. Because we have learned who it is all for is worth it.

A way Jesus demonstrated sacrifice is through His acts of service. While He was the rightful ruler of all, He often humbled Himself to the standing a servant. Just a week before He knew He would be betrayed and crucified, Jesus knelt at His disciples' feet and washed them. He literally got His hands dirty so that His disciples, and eventually we, could witness an excellent example of what it means to sacrifice our self-regard and serve.

Jesus often showed the ability to sacrifice whatever was necessary in order to bring glory to His Father. Whether that would be going out of His way to have a transformational encounter with a Samaritan woman at a well to simply being content traveling with no valuable earthly possessions, Jesus showed living a life in pursuit of sacrificing for others was possible.

But what does that look like for us today? While I cannot answer for everyone reading this, I do know opportunities to serve and sacrifice exist all around. For me, I sacrifice my time and money to buy breakfast for the younger men in my life who are trying to follow after Christ. They might find it annoying that I refuse to let them take the bill, but I am more than willing to pay if it means they have come to a greater understanding of their faith through our morning coffee shop conversations.

For you, sacrifice could be allowing others to interrupt your schedule so you can share the Gospel with them, or it could mean sacrificing some lifestyle decisions so that you are not causing those around you to stumble. As Romans

14 discusses, we must not participate in those actions which will cause our fellow brothers and sisters in Christ to fall from the path the Lord has set before them.

You might be 21 and drink a few drinks without getting drunk, but maybe your friend lacks the self-control to be in the presence of alcohol without becoming completely wasted. Are you willing to sacrifice your drinking habits so your friend can stay sober-minded?

Or perhaps you can watch an R-rated film without it affecting your thoughts, but your friend struggles with lust and sexual temptation. Will you sacrifice in this area of your life for the sake of others?

Maybe you have been called to sacrifice even more than this. Maybe you have been called to serve in our nation's armed forces or have been shown you are to take the Gospel to China and the Far-Eastern world which are fervently against the Christian message. Whatever the case, do you have the confidence and boldness to declare "Jesus, I will follow you... no matter the cost."

Being honest with you, many seasons in my life, I struggle to bring myself to this declaration. I let my sin and fear convince me I am inadequate to follow Christ. I convince myself I need my sin and fear to live a fulfilling and satisfying life. I am convinced my comfort, time, relationships, and social standing are too valuable to surrender to God. I begin to idolize the creation instead of worshipping the Creator.

So how did I go from a man overly consumed with my sin to a man willing to sacrifice hundreds of hours to write this book? Needless to say, I had a lot of help.

God placed people in my life who spoke certain truths to me at the proper moments for me to realize I was not living the life I have been called to. Certain storms blew into my life which revealed to me the things I idolized would not sustain me. And most importantly, the Holy Spirit made my heart soft and spoke words of conviction opening my eyes to the reality of how much more fulfilling my life could be by sacrificing my everything. It seems contradictory and illogical, but as Luke 9:24 states:

> "If you try to hang on to your life, you will lose it. But if you give up your life for my sake, you will save it."

We find ourselves, by sacrificing ourselves. Does that make sense? Probably as much sense as Advanced College Calculus makes to non-mathematicians. But just because we do not understand something does not make it less true. And just because we do not understand this particular topic, does not mean we can't understand the components of the very same idea.

Many people reading this would probably understand the numbers, operations, and perhaps even the algebra that goes into proofs of Advanced Calculus. So also, can we know the truths that our God is a perfect God and we are sinners prone to mess things up. Therefore, why not surrender everything to the One who can be trusted with the well-being of the entire universe? Now phrased like this, Luke 9 becomes the only logical action.

Back to the question above – are you able to say you will follow Jesus no matter what? Think on this as you read the following story. It is about a pilot named John Ferrier who recognized what the scope of sacrifice could entail...

On the morning of June 7, 1958, the Minute Men, an air demonstration team of the Air National Guard, were performing a show above the suburb outside Dayton, Ohio. The pilots were successfully completing formation after formation without flaw. The crowds were amazed. Later in the show the leader of the Sabrejet team, Colonel Williams, called for the planes to turn their smoke trails on and then the diamond of planes all pulled up into the clear blue sky.

Suddenly, the four ships split apart, rolling to the four points of a compass leaving a flower like pattern. On the ground below the crowd gazed at the remarkable work of art. Then everything changed. One of the pilots, John Ferrier, had lost control of his plane and it was rolling towards a small town named Fairborn.

As the other pilots realized this, they immediately broke formation and raced after their companion. Williams radioed to Ferrier, "Bailout, John! Get out of there!" Captain Ferrier still had plenty of time to eject safely but didn't. Williams issued twice more his command but each time the only response was a blip of smoke from the out-of-control plane.

The message was clear to the other pilots... John couldn't reach the mike button because he was tugging on the control stick trying to regain control of his craft. The only thing he could do was send a smoke message since the smoke button was on the stick. As the plane neared the houses of Fairborn, John's actions became clear. He was holding out to save the town below.

A terrible explosion then shook the earth before a deafening silence. Williams called out, "Johnny? Are you there? Captain, answer me!" No response. The remaining airborne planes raced back the Air Force base to land and drove to the site of the crash. When arriving they found a warlike scene with Captain Ferrier's plane crashed between four houses – the only place that a crash could have occurred without killing any of the residences. The explosion knocked down a woman and a few children, but no one had been hurt; except for Johnny who had been killed on impact.

An elderly man who resided in the town of reported that, "When the plane started to roll, he was heading straight for us. For a second (my family) looked right at each other. This was the end. Then, he pulled up right over us and put it in there. This man died for us."

A few days after the accident, Tulle Ferrier, John's wife, found a worn card in his billfold with the words "I'm Third". That phrase summed up Johnny's life and death. To him these few words were the reason he sacrificed his life for complete strangers. God was first, others were second, and he was third.

This "I'm Third" philosophy is the governing principle at one of the most impactful places of my childhood, Kanakuk Kamps.[‡] To put God first, others second, and yourself third, or as I described it back in chapter 1, JOY, is the greatest way I know of to be reminded to continually be living a life of sacrifice.

Living to be third, "shooting for the bronze" in our everyday walks, will cause others to look at us strange, but what better opportunity is there to share the Gospel with them when they undoubtably ask why it is we do what we do!

We must be content in sacrificing our plans, dreams, desires, and pleasures for the sake of others and for the sake of Christ. And if God calls upon us to make the ultimate sacrifice of our lives, we must pray that we have the strength to follow through. Just as Anna did for Elsa,

---

[‡] It is at this camp where I learned the story of John Ferrier. In honor of the captain's sacrifice, Kanakuk named its most prestigious camper award after him.

just as Capitan Ferrier did for complete strangers, and just as Jesus did for us.

Sacrifice is difficult but like the topic of love I discussed last chapter, the pursuit of this ideal is noble and worthwhile. Not to mention when you pursue one, naturally the other will follow. John 15:10-13 reads:

> *When you obey my commandments, you remain in my love, just as I obey my Father's commandments and remain in his love. I have told you these things so that you will be filled with my joy. Yes, your joy will overflow! This is my commandment: Love each other in the same way I have loved you. There is no greater love than to lay down one's life for one's friends.*

Let us lay our everything down. Let us lay it all at the foot of the cross and let Christ decide what it is He wants to use. When we give our everything to God, when we humbly declare everything we have is from Him, we allow the opportunity of a great change to occur. Living out our purpose becomes easier and serving others become second nature.

All of us are called to sacrifice, the question we need to answer is what is God calling you specifically to lay down in order to glorify Him? Not all of us will be called to die for our faith, but if you are, do you have faith enough to lay down your life like your Savior? Will you act in love for a friend, for a brother or sister, and take the sword meant for someone else so they can experience a glimpse of what Christ did for them? Will you settle for bronze in this race called life letting God have the gold and others have the silver?

This only happens if you are madly in love with Jesus. For if you are not in love with Him, there is no chance you will be able to surrender your comfort, time, or money, let alone your life. And to fall madly in love with Jesus, just look to the grandest symbol of sacrifice of all history. As Billy Graham puts it, "The cross shows us the seriousness of our sin—but it also shows us the immeasurable love of God."§

Is this not what sacrifice is? For sacrifice is achieved at its highest level through love. And unlike the end of last chapter, there is no ... needed here.

---

§ From Billy Graham's *Wisdom for Each Day.*

RILEY'S STORY

I'm writing this exactly 46 days from my wedding, and I am terrified. Yes, there are all the anxieties of the wedding day and the many things that go into its preparation, but mostly I'm terrified that I don't have what it takes to be the husband my wonderful future wife deserves.

In Ephesians, Paul writes that husbands should love their wives "just as Christ loved the church and gave himself up for her." That last part is something to wonder about. What does it mean to "give myself up" for my wife? If I were to ask any happily married man, he would gladly take a bullet for his wife, and many will tell you that: both as an answer and as their interpretation of this passage. And many will tell you that while simultaneously turning up the T.V. to drown out the sound of their wives talking. Is Biblical sacrifice simply a willingness to die for someone you love?

I know I speak out of this weird existence of pre-marriage naivety, but a willingness to die for your wife seems too easy. Anyone would tell you that; I mean, I would even tell you that, and I am not married. I think Paul is asking much more from us in this case. When Christ "gave himself up" for the Church, I see the Him as a man devoting His entire human life to nurturing His Church. If Christ "giving himself up" for the Church simply meant dying for her, Christianity would be a rather confusing religion of people worshiping some guy who died on a cross without ever giving a reason for His time on Earth or for His death.

Jesus sacrificed more than His life: He sacrificed His whole self. Jesus sacrificed His time, His comforts, His power, His needs and even His eternal relationship with the Father and the Holy Spirit during His time on the cross. There is a clear difference between a willingness to die for something, and a willingness to live for it: Jesus knew this well.

Jesus lived and died for His Church, and that is what I believe Paul means for husbands to give themselves up for their wives just as Christ loved the Church. Ask me if I would die for my future wife, and every second of every day I will tell you "yes" no matter the circumstances; but, ask me to give up my time, my comfort, my interests, my lusts, my energy, my desires, and my priorities? I don't know if I would have an answer for you. I don't know if I'm ready for that. I don't know if I'll ever be able to sacrifice myself, to give up both my life and everything that lives in it, for my wife.

But I do know a Savior who gave Himself up perfectly, both in life and in death, for His bride. This same Savior pours His love into me, by way of His Holy Spirit, so that I, too, may love. From Christ, I know a sacrificial love that gives up anything and everything for me, and in Christ, I am able to love a sacrificial love that will give up anything and everything for my future wife.

-CHAPTER 9-

A STORY OF COMPANIONSHIP

Throughout human history there have been days that will be remembered forever. Some days, like December 7, 1941 or September 11, 2001 will be recalled as moments of great tragedy. Some days, like July 4, 1776 or November 11, 1918 will be celebrated as moments of terrific victory. While some days, like that of July 20, 1969 will be look upon as days of remarkable achievement. And among these days of achievement, I believe one must not be overlooked. For this day I believe measures up to that of a moon-landing moment... namely, let us remember October 12, 2019.

Why this day one might ask? What sets this particular Saturday apart from all other days? Specifically, it was on this day in history where man achieved new limits to how far it can push itself. On this day Eliud Kipchoge became the first man to run a sub 2-hour marathon.

For those reading this who might not be into sports or a fan of running, this achievement might confuse you as to why it is so monumental. Prior to this point, many doctors, athletes, and reporters were convinced running a marathon in under 2 hours was next to impossible. It would require one athlete to push their body past the point it had ever gone before. They thought it was anatomically unreason-able to expect this of anyone. Eliud was out to prove the doubters wrong... and prove them wrong he did.

Because he refused to let the expectations of others dictate what he could and could not do, Eliud is set to go down as perhaps the greatest long-distance runner in history. And with that October 12 will be forever engraved into the record books. However, I do not believe the sole reason this day should be remembered is due to this record being broken. Nor do I believe it should only be Eliud celebrated on this day. Rather, I am convinced October 12 will go down as one of the greatest demonstrations of teamwork ever.

Now this will puzzle most everyone reading this. Are marathons not an individual endeavor? Was it not Eliud who had to break the 2-hour mark on his own? To quote the runner himself, "100% of me is nothing compared to 1% of the whole team. That's teamwork." Even he realized his achievement was that of a group and not an individual.

For in order to reach the goal, Eliud was supported by a world-class team who assembled for the sole purpose of achieving the impossible. From coaches, nutritionists, physiotherapists, and a pace car complete with futuristic lasers, no aspect was overlooked to accomplish this goal. But of all the things that helped Eliud during his run, none were more important than the over 40 pacemakers running beside him.

Rotating out every 5 to 10 kilometers, Eliud had constant support of other world-class athletes set on helping him reach this mark. They included former world recorder holders, multiple major marathon first place runners, Olympic gold medalists, and college national champions. While none of these individuals ran the whole race, without them Eliud would likely have never finished with the time he did.

And is this not the same with us in life? In the marathon we are running, would we finish if we did not have the support of those around us? Where would we be if not for the friends and families we have been blessed with – no matter how many or how few?

For that reason, October 12 is of so great importance, because it reminds us that we are nothing without a team. We might be able to limp through life on our own, but without the support of others it will be difficult to finish well.

I have once heard it said we are the sum of our five closest friends. Whoever we spend the most time with and talk to the most will ultimately influence who we become and how we will run the race of life before us. Looking at just my life, I find evidence this claim largely holds true. But if I could make one adjustment to this remark, I am not sure "friend" would be my chosen word to use. Because if I said my growth towards God due to the influence of others stops with friendship, then I would be lying.

Friends do play a major role, but they are not alone. Just as Eliud needed pacemakers and doctors, so also do we need a wide assortment of people in our journeys. This is why this chapter is titled companionship rather than friendship, for I believe companionship encompasses much, much more.

We are not just the sum of our five closest friends with regards to our spiritual walk. We are meant to have a diverse team around us guiding us closer and closer to our Father above. Throughout the next pages, it is this team I wish to explore.

To do this, I will focus on four unique roles people can play in your life and you can play in the lives of others.

These are Four W's of Spiritual Teams: Walkers, Watchmen, Workmen, and Warriors.*

Walkers:

The first component of this championship spiritual team is the walker. Simply put, the walker on the team is you! Before constructing the support system around you, you first must be committed to walking the spiritual journey yourself. You must decide to walk with Christ in all your endeavors if any other relationships in your life will hold any meaning.

Without the most important relationship solidified, namely the relationship between you and God, then it will not matter who you have around you. Your faith is your faith and while others can help nurture it and grow it, they cannot hold your faith for you.

The passionate, personal pursuit of Jesus is necessary. How can we test to see if we are fulfilling our role as Walker? An answer can be found in 1 John 2:3-6:

> *And we can be sure that we know him if we obey his commandments. If someone claims, "I know God," but doesn't obey God's commandments, that person is a liar and is not living in the truth. But those who obey God's word truly show how completely they love him. That is how we know we are living in him. Those who say they live in God should live their lives as Jesus did.*

When we are living our lives like that of how Jesus did, we are a true Walker. When we are purpose-driven and chasing authenticity, we are walking. For if we are not filling

---

* Adapted from Dan Britton's Wisdom Walks: Sports Edition.

ourselves up first, if we are not taking care of our own spiritual well-being, then we will be useless in pouring out into others. As this passage implies, our public impact directly correlates to our private devotion.

Our walk will not be simple. There will be obstacles placed on our path to trip us up, but as Hebrews 12:1 commands us – we are to run this race with endurance. We are to endure the trials, tribulations, and hardships of life and keep walking.

When faced with persecution, we pray. When worry seeks to engulf us, we worship. When society feeds us lies, we pause and listen. In our restlessness, we read the Word. In all circumstances, we desire to abide in the comfort of our Lord.

Unfortunately, this is all easier to write than it is to actually do. Many times, we will allow ourselves to get caught up in the gravity of the obstacles before us. We stop walking. Galatians 5:7 asks us in these situations, *"You were running the race so well. Who has held you back from following the truth?"* And the answer to this "who" question is typically ourselves.

The only person who can keep us from being in relationship with God is ourselves. No one else can keep us from worship, prayer, and daily engagement with our Lord. That is why if we look deeper at the obstacles placed in our life, we will discover some of them to be placed there by our own actions. When we arrive at this realization, we must hear the words of Paul just a few verses later:

> So I say, let the Holy Spirit guide your lives. Then you won't be doing what your sinful nature craves.
>
> Galatians 5:16

137

At all moments of our walk, we should let the Spirit be our guide. We must allow the Spirit to guide us in ways of love, joy, peace, patience, kindness, goodness, faithfulness, gentleness, and self-control. Only when we are doing this will the next three relationships be most beneficial. Only when we are a Walker, locked arm in arm with Jesus Christ, can we experience true growth from the other relationships in our lives.

Watchmen:

Perhaps the greatest way we can grow in knowledge and wisdom within our spiritual journey is by having a caring and strong Watchman. This person is that of a mentor in our lives. They are a teacher with more spiritual life experience than we have.

Normally the watchman is an older man or woman walking the same path we are walking except they are just farther down the road. While it is not required for them to be older, an effective Watchman will always be more mature in the faith than the Walker they are leading.

A key role of this position is they are willing and able to pass down real-life advice and wisdom which they have picked up along their own journey. The Watchman is open with their own past mistakes so we can avoid the same blunders. Ultimately, to see a great example of what this relationship looks like, look no farther than Paul and Timothy within Scripture.

Paul was the Watchman to his spiritual son, Timothy. As seen throughout Paul's correspondence with Timothy, Paul was mentoring Timothy by equipping him for the tasks of ministry. By challenging and encouraging Timothy, Paul empowered his young protégé with the tools to spread the Gospel message. And Paul continually reminded Timothy of his commitment to share this message. By providing wisdom from his own life experiences and truth from Scripture, Paul invested into future generations by investing into Timothy.

How Paul was with Timothy, so also should our Watchman be with us. They are there to challenge us to discover a deeper understanding of who God is and where our purpose lies. We should have a high level of admiration, respect, and gratitude for this individual in our lives for they are sacrificing much in order to pour into us.

Not only are Watchmen concerned with their own Spiritual journeys, but they are involved in building ours. When we pause on our walks, they are there to help pull us forward. As Proverbs 13:20 reads:

> *Walk with the wise and become wise; associate with fools and get in trouble.*

We have the opportunity to learn from our mentors and implement weather-tested practices. But we must be careful in identifying who fits this role in our lives. We must avoid the fool. For if they are blind in their own walk with Christ, then they will likely be leading us along the same wrong path they are walking.

When discovering our Watchman, we must pray for the discernment to recognize genuine spiritual maturity. A great way to find this is to find those individuals in our lives who have the boldness and confidence to mimic Paul's remarks in 1 Corinthians 11:1: *"And you should imitate me, just as I imitate Christ."*

Paul did not hesitate to tell those who were reading his writing to imitate his walk with the Lord. Paul recognized younger Christians needed an example to follow and he was willing to be that example. But how often today are people unwilling to take on this burden and say, "Don't look at me, look at Jesus."

While this sentiment is true, it appears to me to be an excuse for lacking the devotion to take on the responsibility of living out our faith. Should people not be seeing Jesus when they look at us? Is not asking others to imitate us not also asking them to imitate Christ if in fact we are truly walking the walk?

And perhaps that is why Paul includes the second part of the verse – *"just as I imitate Christ."* Paul knew it was not he who was worthy to be the example, but rather it was 'Paul, follower of Jesus' who was the example. This is the mindset our Watchmen in life should have. They should be bold and declare 1 Corinthians 11:1 to us with the understanding we are to only follow them as much as we see them following Christ.

Our mentor, our Watchman, guides us on right paths by sharing God's Word. And as Paul challenged Timothy, so also our Watchman challenges us:

> *Let no one despise you for your youth, but set*
> *the believers an example in speech, in conduct,*
> *in love, in faith, in purity.*
>
> 1 Timothy 4:12 (ESV)

Workman:

Just as the Watchman is someone investing into us, the Workman is someone we are investing into. As we are having wisdom be poured into us, we should be pouring out that wisdom into others.

We have been given a mission to make disciples of all nations and having a Workman walking behind us is a great way to fulfill this calling. Once again looking at Paul and Timothy as an example, we see Paul was not content with

Timothy just sitting on the knowledge he had learned. Rather Paul instructed Timothy to share his message.

You have heard me teach things that have been confirmed by many reliable witnesses. Now teach these truths to other trustworthy people who will be able to pass them on to others.

2 Timothy 2:2

Effective Watchmen and Workmen relationships have a never-ending ripple effect. The Watchman instructs their Workman only for the Workman to become the Watchman of another Workman... and the patterns continues.

In my life, I have been blessed to have many Workmen look to me as a mentor and spiritual leader. And in these relationships, not only have I seen them grow in their faith, but I have been challenged to grow in my own. For I believe it is in our nature to avoid being seen as a hypocrite, therefore when we are actively discipling someone, we are challenged to live out the things we are preaching to them. We are tasked with living truth while we teach truth.

I discovered this reality in a relationship with a younger man I mentored and continue to mentor. His name is Sam. When I first became friends with Sam, I instantly recognized many of the same traits in his life as in my life.

I saw a desire to grow closer to God and influence others for the Kingdom of Heaven, but I also saw a man caught up with societal standards and temptations. He essentially was a younger me.

Through years of getting to know him better, I eventually was given the opportunity to see Sam take on the role of Workman in my life. What started as merely training him to take over a leadership position I held in high school, became a relationship where I was able to share Scripture and life experiences with him well into my college years. While I hope he has learned many things from me, I at least know I have learned much from him.

By listening to the questions he asked and taking time to answer with Scripture, I grew in maturity and in ability to share the Gospel message effectively. Sam has taught me the importance of investing into others for through him I have seen many others come to know Christ.

How? Because Sam is genuinely devoted to growing in his spiritual journey, he recognized early the importance of mentoring others in his life. He reaches individuals which would be difficult for me to reach because he had relationships with them that I did not. This is the beauty of having a Workman in life... we get to see the impact of our actions on the next generation of believers.

What about those of you who may be convinced you lack the spiritual knowhow to mentor someone else in faith? My encouragement to you is this – no matter what stage of your journey you are on, it is always a great time to be investing into someone.

If the extent of your knowledge is "Jesus loves you," then find someone in your life who does not know that truth and share it with them. If you believe to be the Paul of your generation, find the believer in your life who has the enthusiasm and willingness to be the next Timothy.

No matter what stage of life you are in, there will always be someone wanting to grow closer to Jesus just a few steps behind you on the path.

Just as your Watchman trains you up in righteousness, train your Workman in the same manner. The greatest investment in life you can make is finding a Workman for unlike all other investments, the return on this investment is eternal.

Warriors:

Of all the W's, I believe the Warrior to be the easiest to identify and explain. For our warriors in life are typically our closest friends. On our spiritual journeys, they are the ones right next to us when we look to our left and right.

Within Warrior relationships there exists an element of mutual mentoring and accountability. They are learning just as much from us as we are from them. It is these relationships to which Proverbs 27:17 refers: *"As iron sharpens iron, so a friend sharpens a friend."*

Warriors bring out the best in each other because they know what causes the other to trip up. No topic of discussion is off limits in these relationships for they value genuine growth and recognize this is only achieved through vulnerability.

One thing I have done with the Warriors I have had in my life is ask each other various Biblically-based questions. These questions helped us celebrate victories in our lives in addition to recognize areas we need to improve.

1. Have I had a devotional time (prayer and Bible study) each day this week? (Ps 119:9-11)
2. Have I thanked God for all the ways He has blessed me recently? (1 Thes 5:18)
3. Have I honored the Lord with the things I've put before my eyes? (Phil 4:8)
4. Have I entertained any fantasy or false intimacy in my life? (2 Cor 10:4-5)
5. Have I shown God to others through my actions and words? (Col 3:17)
6. Have I hidden any conflict or struggle from God or from my peers? (2 Tim 1:8)
7. Have I been completely honest in my answers to the above questions? (Col 3:9)

Yes, these are some tough questions, and at points giving honest answers was next to impossible. But my friends and I realized in order to strengthen our relationships with the Lord, we had to be willing to talk about more than just sports or the weather.

We sought growth and these questions demonstrated our commitment to such growth. And despite these friends knowing my full self completely, they still sought to love me unconditionally. In my life, they were the soldiers who would through themselves on the grenades life threw at me because they know I would do the same for them.

In the book of Mark, we read of a great account of four men who fulfilled their role of Warrior for their friend. We see they put their schedules on hold so that they can help a brother experience Jesus.

When Jesus returned to Capernaum several days later, the news spread quickly that he was back home. Soon the house where he was staying was so packed with visitors that there was no more room, even outside the door. While he was preaching God's word to them, four men arrived carrying a paralyzed man on a mat. They couldn't bring him to Jesus because of the crowd, so they dug a hole through the roof above his head. Then they lowered the man on his mat, right down in front of Jesus. Seeing their faith, Jesus said to the paralyzed man, "My child, your sins are forgiven... Stand up, pick up your mat, and go home!"

And the man jumped up, grabbed his mat, and walked out through the stunned onlookers.

Mark 2:1-5, 11-12

These four men were willing to go to extremes for their friend to experience the miracle he was waiting on. Their attitude should be the example attitude our Warriors have for us and we have for our fellow Warriors. No matter what the cost – inconvenience, public humiliation, discomfort – Warriors are ready to march onto battle for one another.

As Ecclesiastes 4:12 reads, "*A person standing alone can be attacked and defeated, but two can stand back-to-back and conquer. Three are even better, for a triple-braided cord is not easily broken.*" This walk we are on, as many of you likely know, is not going to be unopposed. There is an enemy who will do all in its power to keep us from running the race before us faithfully. But with Warriors... with true friends locked arm and arm with you, our battle becomes easier.

If I were to pause here and ask you, "in your opinion what makes a friend a good friend?" I would likely receive many responses. However, I am convinced one answer would show up more often than most. Namely, I believe many would respond by saying a good friend is with you no matter what... a good friend can confidently proclaim "I am for you."

A good friend will help you achieve your dreams and endeavors. They will not stand against you unless you are heading down a path towards destruction.

Our Warriors in life exists to point us to Jesus in our distress, not to focus on our sin. Yes, they should call it out when they see it, but then they return to a position of encouragement. They encourage us to walk faithfully once more just as we do the same with them.

How can you see if someone is a good Warrior? Do they follow Jesus and are growing in His ways? Do they demonstrate great integrity in all things? Do they remain close even in the tough times? Do you consider them a great friend? If all these things are true, consider talking with this individual about becoming Warriors for each other.

But be careful not to seek too many Warriors. Not every friend you have needs to be as invested into your spiritual well-being as your Warriors are. Not all your friends will make great Warriors.

Proverbs 18:24 states, *"There are 'friends' who destroy each other, but a real friend sticks closer than a brother."* Find these real friends. Lock into one or two true Warriors to do life with.

Remember, even Jesus had His go to inner circle of Peter, James, and John. With them He had a deeper level of trust and closeness than compared to the other disciples. Why should we not seek the same in our relationships?

◊ ◊ ◊ ◊ ◊

The great thing about the Four W's of Spiritual Teams is the fact we will play every role at any given time. Obviously, we will always be fulfilling the role of Walker. When we are mentored by our Watchman, we fulfill the role of Workman. In the seasons we are discipling others, we fulfill the role of Watchman. And when we decide to run our spiritual race with friends to our left and right, we naturally fulfill the role of Warrior for those running beside us.

Recognize however, with all these relationships, ends are likely evident. For the saying "There are friends for a season, friends for a reason, and friends for a lifetime" holds true in all these positions on your Spiritual Team.

Perhaps a Watchman was in your life just to get you through a storm you were in. Maybe someone is your Workman just long enough for you to depart one great piece of wisdom upon them. And possibly there is one Warrior in your life that you believe to be there for a lifetime that will be taken away from you – by an untimely death or by simply growing apart. Whatever the case might be, always keep in mind the point of these relationships in the first place.

The goal of mentorships, discipleship, and friendships is to bring all involved closer to God. Therefore, be open to the possibility of allowing God to break apart a relationship so that more people can experience Him.

As we read about in Acts 15 with Paul and Barnabas, sometimes the best thing for the spread of the Gospel is when inseparable Warriors go separate ways. Now instead of a single superstar team sharing the Good News, there now was two – Mark and Barnabas sailing off in one direction and Paul and Silas venturing in the other.

We don't know how much time we have before we are called home. Therefore, let us appreciate the relationships in our lives while we have them. Let us build our team of world-class Christians now in order to make today the day we conquered the marathon of our lives.

SYDNEY'S STORY

From the beginning of my time at college, I have been blessed and challenged in many ways. The night before I moved into my dorm freshman year, I remember having the thought: how am I going to find people like me? How am I going to keep up with my faith in this new and overwhelming environment? Little did I know the plans God had to transform me over the next four years.

I'm not going to lie, over the first two years of college I was not as connected or involved with my faith as I was leaving high school. I frequently drove home on Sundays to go to church with my mom and I loved that, but I felt still like something was missing.

My junior year is really when I first felt a transformation happening. One of the football players wanted to start having Fellowship of Christian Athletes meetings and I was all for it. After a few weeks of planning and inviting people, we went from not having an FCA on campus to over 50 students becoming involved. This organization gave me a built-in excuse to share my faith and connect with people on campus who were seeking the same thing I sought. God provided me a great faith-based community, the very thing I was searching for.

My senior year brought a lot of tears and temptations, but because of the faith community that surrounded me, I had peers around me who I could turn to. I knew they would always be there for me because we are all walking through this thing called life with Christ. That time of struggle strengthened me and through it I made even more connections that I thought possible. I also began to notice that I was more confident when I talked to others about my faith. I was no longer worried if they were 'like me' in having faith or not like I was concerned with my first two years. I simply showed them kindness and always left the invitation wide open to come to FCA or church and talk about Jesus.

I learned there are really two paths people can take when they go into college (or begin any new chapter in their lives for that fact). They can fall to temptations and expectations and abandon faith or they can decide to go all in for Jesus. While we can't control everything that happens, we can control who we surround ourselves with. Surround ourselves with strong believers, and we can expect to grow our spiritual strength.

God used my college experience to teach me lessons that no one else could. I was concerned that in a college environment, I had to be a certain way. I was not confident enough to share my faith until God put people in my life who showed me that it was okay to be different. They were my example my junior year, and the real transformation came my senior year when I realized I was being called to be that same example for others. I needed to be that example for the underclassmen that I never had.

Through people God put in my life and involvement in a faith-community, I have seen God mold me into a woman I am proud to be today. It took a lot of sacrifice and determination on my side and even more grace and mercy on God's part for me to experience the transformation I did. But I'm the best version of myself at this point in my life – and the best is yet to come.

-CHAPTER 10-

A STORY OF URGENCY

Luke 10 details the story of Christ sending out His disciples into the world to share the message He had given them. Within this story, we observe Christ's instructions were laced with a sense of urgency. There was a job needing to be done and Christ knew of how little time there was to complete it...

> These were his instructions to them: "The harvest is great, but the workers are few. So pray to the Lord who is in charge of the harvest; ask him to send more workers into his fields. Now go and remember that I am sending you out as lambs among wolves. Don't take any money with you, nor a traveler's bag, nor an extra pair of sandals. And don't stop to greet anyone on the road.
>
> Whenever you enter someone's home, first say, 'May God's peace be on this house.' If those who live there are peaceful, the blessing will stand; if they are not, the blessing will return to you. Don't move around from home to home. Stay in

one place, eating and drinking what they provide. Don't hesitate to accept hospitality, because those who work deserve their pay.

If you enter a town and it welcomes you, eat whatever is set before you. Heal the sick, and tell them, 'The Kingdom of God is near you now.' But if a town refuses to welcome you, go out into its streets and say, 'We wipe even the dust of your town from our feet to show that we have abandoned you to your fate. And know this—the Kingdom of God is near!'"

Luke 10:2-11

This story provides us great insight into what living on mission looks like in addition to what it means to live with an attitude of urgency. Not just urgency to share the Gospel, but also urgency to grow in faith and urgency to deal with sin.

However, recognize this urgency we are to have is not that as it is typically defined by society. Society associates being urgent with having a "go, go, go mindset." We are to hurry to complete the task we have been given – time is of the essence. But this is not what we witness Scripture to command.

Having a Biblical sense of urgency means we move quickly but do not rush. We allow for the adequate amount of time to fully devote our attention to the job at hand. And even before we begin, we take a moment to stop. As seen within the first verse of the above passage, Jesus instructs His disciples to pray prior to departing. Urgency then can be said to start in a state of stillness.

For many of us, this might seem illogical and counter-cultural. How can being still accomplish the jobs that need to be done and the mission we have been given? On the

3

A Story of Urgency

surface, I would tend to agree with you. However, digging deeper reveals moments of stillness are actually extremely common within our "go, go, go" culture.

Before the snap of the ball in football, the tip-off in basketball, the shot of the gun in track, or the delivery of a pitch in baseball, there exists a moment of stillness. It is a check to make sure everyone is ready to begin. Without this moment, athletes would struggle to be mentally prepared to take on the challenges that come through competition. And this moment extends beyond the arena of athletics.

Before a musician begins playing a piece, they compose themselves with a deep breath. Before a soldier goes into battle, they sit in solidarity, mentally checking that they are ready to fight. Before a doctor begins a surgery, they stand in silence, allowing their expertise and wisdom the opportunity to take control. In fact, I would venture to say before departing on any task of any level of importance, it is essential that at least a second of stillness occurs beforehand.

Spiritually, the same holds true. We have been given a monumental mission to complete. Therefore, we must discipline ourselves before we begin our "game", "song", "battle", or "operation" to take a moment of stillness. This allows us to gather ourselves and refocus on the "why" behind our actions.

This moment is vital to knowing what it is we are to do. As Psalm 46:10 says, *"Be still and know..."* Discovering the purpose behind our actions becomes known when we stop and pray, read Scripture, mediate, journal, or sit in solitude. And when we know, we then can grow.

As followers of Christ, if we are to be effective in our going, we must be faithful in constantly growing. And a great way to be growing, is to apply the wisdom we discover within our moments of stillness. Unfortunately, Christians today are known more for their complacency than their activities. For while we might know a lot, we do not do a lot. Just imagine, if we were to apply just half of the things we have learned during our walks with Christ, how different our world would be!

> *There is much more we would like to say about this, but it is difficult to explain, especially since you are spiritually dull and don't seem to listen. You have been believers so long now that you ought to be teaching others. Instead, you need someone to teach you again the basic things about God's word. You are like babies who need milk and cannot eat solid food. For someone who lives on milk is still an infant and doesn't know how to do what is right. Solid food is for those who are mature, who through training have the skill to recognize the difference between right and wrong.*
>
> *Hebrews 5:11-14*

Are we stagnant in our faith, relying constantly on spiritual milk rather than meat? Urgency means we are not satisfied with staying as a spiritual infant. We wish to mature to greater responsibilities and knowledge. And we do this by taking the lessons of our stillness and applying them during our battle. We have grown in order to be well equipped to go.

Now as we go, we must have urgency within the midst our going. As Luke 10:4 above states, *"Don't take any money with you, nor a traveler's bag, nor an extra pair of sandals. And don't stop to greet anyone on the road."* In other words, don't let any of your possessions in your life tie you down. And more simply put – do not waste time!

154

This passage is not calling for us to drop everything and become a nomadic monk, nor is it a formula to be rude to the people in our lives. Rather Jesus here is telling us to get on with the task He has given us. We are not to be distracted by material concerns nor by tedious ceremonies of etiquette. Urgency requires us to use our time wisely, therefore letting things that have no eternal value hold us back have no place in our lives.

And one of the things that we must choose to leave behind on our journey is the sin tying us to our past. We must decide to make the changes we need now in order for us to avoid self-sabotage on our journey later. These decisions do not need to be earth-shattering but can be small commitments to correct our course to align with the calling of Christ. Instead of a complete change in trajectory, let us make one-degree alterations. Let me explain what I mean with the following illustration...

If NASA were to send a rocket to the moon and it was only one-degree off at launch, after one mile of flight the rocket would be 92 feet off course. No big deal, right? But at this rate, the rocket would never arrive at the moon. It would be 4,169 miles off course.* If this same rocket, were heading to the nearest star, it would end up 441 billion miles off target. One-degree makes a huge difference.

Negatively, this means small compromises to temptations now, could mean big trouble later. Positively, however, this means small adjustments, commitments, and wise decisions now, could mean a world of difference in the future. Significant growth in relationships, in maturity, and in wisdom is not attained quickly. It comes by making the right small decision today.

---

* This is equivalent to approximately the distance between the southeastern tip of Florida and the far-western Aleutian island in Alaska.

Want to remain faithful in your marriage? Commit now to having eyes only for the person God has in store for you. Want to overcome an addiction? Begin today by creating a network of accountability. Want to see your friend come to Christ? Start praying for them in this moment.

This all sounds so obvious and basic. But how often do we make the wrong one-degree changes in life and find ourselves in a place we thought we would never be? How often do we waste opportunities to make these small adjustments and discover we are walking a path we did not agree to walk? Trust me, the small changes we make now will echo into eternity.

Therefore, let us commit to not wasting the time we have been given. Let us not be tied down by sin or worldly responsibilities. Instead, let us urgently proclaim the Good News that is the Gospel. Let us urgently press on towards the prize worth fighting for – namely, a greater understanding of the love our Lord has for us. We only have a limited amount of time, so let's not waste it!

Luke 10:9 tells that *"the kingdom of God is near."* It is a warning and reminder of the limited amount of time we have to complete the mission we have been given and to make the changes we need to make.

Life is full of uncertainties, but one thing we can all know with absolute certainty is this – we will die. We are only here for a limited amount of time before our Father will call us home. With every second that passes, we become closer to our death than our birth. This is a huge reason we must live with urgency.

> *This is all the more urgent, for you know how late it is; time is running out. Wake up, for our salvation is nearer now than when we first believed.*
>
> *Romans 13:11*

It seems like I am reminded of this fact far too often. As a sophomore in college, I received news that a man I become friends with at an FCA camp had passed away. Apparently one night he decided that he had enough of this life and sped his car straight off the road into a tree.

Two years later, as I sat tutoring someone in math, I was sent a text saying another friend of mine had a tragic accident. There was an unintentional discharge of a gun, and sadly his life was lost.

I have had older relatives die before, but these two events affected me differently. Two young men with their whole life ahead of them were taken far too early. Unfortunately, I realize I am not alone in these experiences. Many of you who are reading this might have similar stories where a friend, a relative, or someone who meant a lot to you met an early end.

Maybe you lost someone because of a drunk driver, a drug overdose, cancer, or any number of tragedies. Whatever the case, in these moments of grief, the world brutally reminds us our time is short. In the blink of an eye, our days can turn from good to bad.

It is experiences like these that provide me the motivation to be purpose-driven... to intentionally seek urgency. For I have been given a life-saving message that must be shared. We never know how much time we or those around us might have left; therefore, let us share with everyone we can the news that through Jesus Christ we might have eternal life. Then, when life here ends, there is no need to express sorrow, but a celebration can begin. For we know as followers of Christ, the end of our journey on earth simply marks the beginning of an adventure in Heaven.

Despite this knowledge however, some people might make excuses for failing to fulfill the purpose we have been given. In terms of sharing the Gospel, the excuse might be that they just do not know how. And this is where the importance of growing in our faith reveals itself once again.

As Hebrews 5 stated earlier, we need to move from mere belief to seeking to teach others. If we are unable to do this, then we need to take a step back in reflection. We must reflect on the true nature of our relationship with our Father. Is it truly a priority or is being Christian just a checkbox we mark off on surveys?

If we are truly seeking relationship with our Lord, then sharing His message is quite simple. For in the moments we do not know what to say, we have the assurance that the Holy Spirit will provide the words needed (Luke 12:12). So, there is no excuse for followers of Christ to not be pursuing opportunities to share the Gospel.

Perhaps though, some will try to make the claim that "I'm waiting on a sign from God before I act." These people are trying to use God as a trump card to get them out of completing the job God Himself has given us to do. Using the language from this chapter, these individuals are refusing to move past the stillness phase of Luke 10. They are mistaking their laziness with spiritual stillness.

The point of being still is not to remain in that state, it is to prepare us to go! Preparation is worthless if there is no performance to follow it up. Preaching the Gospel to those who need to hear it will never be the wrong move. So, what are you waiting for? If a sign from God is all you need, then consider me your divine messenger because He has sent me to tell you to GO!†

But why go now when I can spend more time in preparation and go later? Can things not change twenty years from now when I am older and wiser? Lord willing,

---

† Reference Mark 16:15, 2 Timothy 4:2, Matthew 10:7, Luke 9:60, Acts 5:20, or really any other multitude of verses.

yes things can still change. Why wait though if God has given you the resources to complete your calling today? For as it is painfully obvious for some of us, tomorrows are not guaranteed. And for those of you who like stats to back up any action you take – here are a few:

> 94% of adult Christians made the decision to follow Christ before the age of 18.
>
> A 25-year-old's chances of accepting Christ are 1 in 5,000.
>
> A 35-year-old's odds of accepting Christ are 1 in 125,000.
>
> And these odds continue to increase every year after...‡

Basically, by the time you are 65, your chances of being saved are so slim that you defy all probabilities if you accept Christ. Your salvation can only be considered as a miracle of grace.

If you are young, these stats make it painstakingly obvious you should be urgently taking the Gospel to your peers for they are more likely to accept it now then later in life. But if you are older reading this, these stats might serve more as a discouragement to you than anything else. The odds of someone believing the message you would take to them are so tiny that there really is no point. Right? Wrong! If anything, I believe these stats serve as greater evidence that we need to have a sense of urgency as we are older. For as we age, it is likely we will encounter more and more individuals who need to hear the Good News of Jesus.

---

‡ Information from the Barna Group and Chuck Smith's Matthew 12 commentary.

And if you say that sharing this news will only lead to them rejecting it, then I must remind you of who it is we serve. We serve a Lord who takes things oddsmakers would view as impossibilities, and He does those things anyways.

I mean what are the odds 300 of Gideon's soldiers could defeat a hundred thousand of the enemy who stood against him? Yet through the power of the Lord, the 300 won.[§] What are the odds that a man born blind will ever see? With God (and some mud), it is 100% certainty.[**] And the odds there could exist a man who could overcome the greatest enemy of us all – death itself? Well, these odds too were overcome by a man called Emmanuel.

> *"O Sovereign Lord! You made the heavens and earth by your strong hand and powerful arm. Nothing is too hard for you!" - Jeremiah 32:17*

> *"What is impossible for people is possible with God." - Luke 18:27*

If you believe it would take a miracle for (fill in the blank) to accept Christ as Lord and Savior, then I am thankful we serve a God of miracles. There is no reason we should not be taking the Good News to the people who need to hear it. And this is the final point of the passage in Luke 10.

Verse 10 and 11 read: *"But if a town refuses to welcome you, go out into its streets and say, 'We wipe even the dust of your town from our feet to show that we have abandoned you to your fate. And know this—the Kingdom of God is near!'"*

[§] I dare you to read this account in Judges 6. It is a much better story than the last stand of the 300 Spartans considering in this story the 300 were victorious.

[**] Reference John 9. I also discussed this story in Chapter 3.

We are to take the Gospel to the everyone needing to hear it, but we need to be aware they do have the freedom to reject this message. The miracle might not happen at the moment we want it to. And if we are faced with rejection, we are not to respond with debate and argument. We simply say our part and if they receive it, we are to rejoice.

If they refuse to hear it, with a heavy heart we must be willing to go elsewhere. Continue to pray for the other individual and continue to show them love in the hopes one day they will have their eyes opened to the truth.

However, if they only express interest in opposing the message we share, we must realize our time can be best spent with others. Our work is to share the news that we have been gifted – mercy through the death of a Savior and salvation through that Savior's resurrection. It is our business to proclaim it and leave it. All the responsibility of receiving or rejecting rests solely on those who hear the message we share.

One way or another, people will discover the price of rejecting Jesus and His Kingdom. For many, this price will not become clear until they are face to face with God on Judgement Day.

But my hope is that God will use my words to reveal to others the magnitude of this price before they reach this Day. I hope through my obedience of sharing an un-sugarcoated account of the Gospel, it will expose to others the urgent need to accept Christ as Savior before it is too late. People need to know that a very real Hell exists, and many good people will end up there because they did not proclaim Jesus as Lord.

My goal is not to scare people into following Jesus but help them recognize a life without Jesus could lead them to a scary existence. I once heard it said, "If I'm wrong about God, then I wasted my life. If you're wrong about God, then you wasted your eternity."†† While I do not fully believe this quote (namely the fact I would argue pursuing a life of love, grace, and forgiveness cannot be considered wasting my life), I do believe it makes a valid point.

People are living life as if there exist no consequences to any of their actions or decisions. We live only to one day turn to dust in a grave. Even if this were true, how bleak an existence that would be!

But if what I believe to be true, namely what the Bible says, is true, then billions are going to be experiencing the consequences of this life's actions for an eternity. That is tough to hear. All the more reason we must live with a sense of urgency to share the message we've been given so the population on the road to hell shrinks.

As Christians, we are in a war! We are in a war for our soul and for the souls around us. Every single moment of every single day our enemy is waiting for the perfect moment to strike in order to knock us off the path God has laid forth before us.

Our enemy is trying to convince us not to fight our sin... not to take the Gospel to our friends and family. He will do everything in his power to keep us from recognizing the victory Christ has achieved on our behalf. Above that, he will do even more to keep us from helping others recognize this victory.

Meanwhile, God is seeking to transform us into the warriors He made us to be. Our Lord knows He is sending us out as sheep amongst wolves, that is why He has provided us access to His strength. Through God's power, we can wage war against the spiritual forces of darkness that battle for our attention.

---

†† Spoken by Christian rapper, Lecrae. Also mimics the famous Pascal's Wager dilemma.

Alone we are weak, but God we can achieve the most unlikely of victories. This life might knock us down, but we urgently rise again. For as true disciples of Christ, if we fall seven times, we will get back up eight.[‡‡]

We will dedicate ourselves to begin our battle with a moment of stillness, so we can recognize where our victory comes from. We will devote ourselves to prayer and the study of Scripture just as many of us devote ourselves to our school, job, relationship, or sport. We do this not because these actions save us, but because we seek spiritual growth in our lives. And we will commit to preaching the Gospel message to all! We declare the war is won through the blood of Jesus Christ!

When we live today like this, then we have truly discovered how to live with a sense of urgency. While we will never know what tomorrow might bring, this urgency provides us with the courage to continue faithfully for we know our forever tomorrow is secured.

Therefore, let us now accept the instructions within Luke 10 as our own. Let us allow Christ to send us out as His disciples in world today. Let us commit to fulfilling our heavenly calling no matter what the cost... for we were not called to stand on the sidelines, but to battle on the frontlines!

[‡‡] Reference Proverbs 24:16

JENNA'S STORY

There are things in life that you hope never will change. The reality of it all, however, is that change is often inevitable. I entered college with a long-term boyfriend and the belief that he would be my rock – the one who would never change or leave my side. I am sure many of you can guess how this story ends up.

The week leading into my junior year, my world came crumbling down. What I had thought to be my most stable and secure relationship had ended. Completely devastated and hurt by this abrupt change, I came to a season in my life when I started to question God. I cannot even begin to count the number of times I asked, "Why God?" Why did this happen? Why now? It was not fair. I felt as if I wasted so much of my energy investing into this relationship for it to end. But as hard as this time was, I recognized it needed to happen.

My ex-boyfriend and I had let sin enter our relationship. It was no longer a relationship rooted in truth as it was when it began. Our focus on Christ and living in a Godly manner was not there anymore. Personally, I had sought satisfaction and approval from someone who was not able to provide those things like Jesus can. When I put that expectation on my significant other, it was bound to lead to disappointment.

These things were all revealed to me as I was walking through the aftermath of this loss. But God was protecting my heart during this troubling time. He was teaching me the value of urgently dealing with the things in my life that were restricting my pursuit of Him while also reminding me of the importance to urgently grow in my faith.

Through this season, I found that I can only find true fulfillment in Christ. It allowed me to understand that I needed to get my relationship right with God before adding another person to my life. God had removed one relationship so that I could see that He is the ONLY One who can fulfill all my expectations.

This journey was a long road, with many tears and many coffee dates with my friends. But through this whole process, God was still working. Whether I could see it or not, He was working! For if it were not for this trial, I would have not grown the way I had. As one of my sisters put it – God was not punishing the Israelites as they went through the desert, He was guiding them to the Promised Land. God was guiding me towards His promises.

This heartache came into my life for a purpose. It opened my eyes and heart to God's unchanging and loving character. He wanted me to lean on Him in the time of change. He sought me to return to a life of seeking Him with urgency. For God's unyielding love was enough for me.

And now, I can glorify His name for the healing and peace He has brought into my life. I can move forward without shame holding me back (1 John 1:9). And I can confidently proclaim to all that Jesus, our Savior, has never left us, never grows weary of us, and will never push us away. Jesus never fails... and that will never change.

-CHAPTER 11-

A STORY OF EXCELLENCE

Throughout Scripture, various metaphors and analogies are used in order to help guide us in our journey called life. One of the most reoccurring of these images are mountains. From Mount Ararat where Noah's ark landed (Genesis 8) to the fact Christ will return on a mountain (Zechariah 14), the Bible clearly spends a lot of time on these enormous landforms.

In the story of Noah's ark, we witness God making a promise to man, sealing it with a rainbow. On Mount Moriah, God demonstrates His faithfulness by providing a substitute for Abraham's son, Isaac (Genesis 22). A divine encounter on Mount Sinai gave Moses God's expectations for His people within the Ten Commandments (Exodus 19-20). Mount Carmel was the site the prophet Elijah proved there was one true God (1 Kings 18). And Mount Olivet became the place our Savior ascended into Heaven with the promise to come again soon.

God used these mountains as places of great teaching and transformation. Ordinary men (with the exception of Jesus), ventured up these great terrains in order to see God in a new way.

While often mountains can be viewed as difficult obstacles one must conquer within life, God reminds us that He is bigger than every Everest in our way. In fact, not only do mountains dwarf in comparison to our Lord, but God will use them to fulfill His plan in our lives. Through mountain-top experiences, God's provision, protection, and promises are on full display.

And don't we all want these mountain-top experiences? Don't we all want the satisfaction and joy that comes while standing on the peak of achievement? Don't we want God to reveal powerful lessons about His character to us?

Christian culture today preaches that we should be striving after our own mountain-top experiences. We should be seeking out a higher spiritual elevation constantly. We should always be climbing.

But this logic confuses me. If we should be reaching for the top of the mountain, then why in most of the stories above does God send his followers right back down the mountain after reaching the top? Is it perhaps because we are not called to live atop a spiritual mountain? Maybe, like Abraham, Moses, and Elijah, we are only to venture up the mountain to gather the wisdom we need to live at the base. Maybe God is calling us to the peak in order to equip us for what lies on the other side of the mountain. And what might that be? A valley.

If mountains are to exist in life, we must also recognize the reality valleys will exist as well – both geographically and metaphorically. In Scripture, the imagery of valleys represents the parts of our life we wish would disappear. It is the sin, the suffering, the heartache, the burden, and the punishment life throws our way. However, just as God used mountains to demonstrate who He is to His followers, so also will He use valleys.

Even when I walk through the darkest valley, I will not be afraid, for you are close beside me. Your rod and your staff protect and comfort me.

Psalm 23:4

When we are in the valleys of life, God will be with us. He will be there to teach us of His power over all and His presence in all. While we might feel down and forgotten, God is there to comfort us.

No matter how deep the valley we are in is, we know there is victory in the end. God will defeat all the evils in our valleys and rescue us from the shackles that might be holding us down.* For our Lord does not call us to have our permanent residence within our valleys.

Mountains and valleys both are significant factors in molding our character into that which is pleasing to our Father. They both serve as great teachers to lessons of trust and perspective. And without their coexistence, the wonders of the mountain can never be fully appreciated nor can the experience of hope within the valleys ever be found. One of my favorite songs drives home this geographical truth so well...

On the mountains, I will bow my life
To the one who set me there
In the valley, I will lift my eyes to the one who sees me there
When I'm standing on the mountain aft, didn't get there on my own
When I'm walking through the valley end, no I am not alone!
You're God of the hills and valleys!

---

* Reference Revelation 16:16-21.

This song, titled *Hills and Valleys* by Tauren Wells, reminds us that the God we serve is over every mountain and every valley. In the peaks of our lives, we are to remember who brought us to our success. And in the valleys, we are to seek the One who can deliver us from our situation. During both the high and low points in life, we ought to be chasing after our Lord.

But since God does not call us to live on mountains, nor does He expect us to live in valleys, where then are we to live? I believe we have been called to live on the ground in between.

In this middle ground we can look down at the valleys and praise God for bringing us up from there. And we can look up to see that God has even more in store for us.

We are to be living in the space where God can use us to help guide people up their mountains, but also where He can use us to help pull people out of their valleys. How will this be accomplished? By pursuing excellence. What does that mean? It means that the way we live is to match that of Christ. And we complete this mission by ultimately setting out to *Be Different*, to *Be Bold*, and to *Be Faithful*.

◊ ◊ ◊ ◊ ◊

As a college student, I have met and witnessed many unique personalities. To me, it seems everyone in college is trying to recreate themselves from high school into new individuals. They are trying to become unlike everyone around them so that people will notice them and seek to become friends with them.

I have seen my peers set out on rebellious routes in order to become someone known on campus. But in all my observations, I have noticed a trend that I guarantee my peers did not count on.

In the pursuit of becoming unlike anyone else, in becoming their own individual, many college students end up as mere clones to those around them. In trying to become different, they ended up becoming the stereotypical college student.

Close friends of mine have decided to abandon their walks with Christ in order to experience the unruly nature college can offer. They thought getting black-out drunk on weekends, having sex with as many people as they could, cussing every other word, and disrespecting authority would be what earned them respect within the larger student population. These actions would ultimately make them "the big man (or woman) on campus."

But for anyone who is currently in college or knows of the college experience, you know it is no longer considered rebellious to drink, do drugs, sleep around, and belittle those around you... it is expected. This life-style is not becoming different but rather the exact opposite. It is conformity.

If the purpose of college is to create free-thinking individuals that will positively contribute to society, then this institution has failed. College today, for a majority of attendees, is a social-conditioning establishment meant to brainwash its clients into conforming to a status quo. While I do not believe universities are intentionally seeking to do this, it is happening, nevertheless. Why? Because people do not want to be different. Romans 12:2 reads:

> *Don't copy the behavior and customs of this world, but let God transform you into a new person by changing the way you think. Then you will learn to know God's will for you, which is good and pleasing and perfect.*

As Christians we are commanded not to conform but to be transformed! A true follower of Christ should be different from their surroundings. Instead of pursuing things society dictates as acceptable and praiseworthy, we as Christians seek the fruits of the Spirit.

We practice love, joy, peace, patience, kindness, goodness, faithfulness, gentleness, and self-control (Galatians 5:22-23). It might be tempting to fall into the enticing deeds society offers, but we recognize that ultimate fulfillment only comes by residing in the Spirit.

That does not mean we might not slip up, but it means we are not making a habit of indulging our sinful desires. At this point another author might pause and provide a list of ways one could go about being different in specific contexts.

Another book might give you 10 ways to make your own fun in college... 10 ways to stand out from your coworkers... 10 ways to not become trapped by the pressures of your peers... 10 ways to (fill in the blank here). But in doing this, I believe we fail to grasp the true issue.

People don't struggle with being different with faith because of some unknown outside force. They struggle due to a lack of knowledge of what being different actually looks like. Instead of being rooted in fact, they base their experiences on feelings. Instead of being moved by the Spirit, they are moved by society. If you want to know what being different truly is, go back and read the first 10 chapters of this book.†

A follower of Christ is reaching for excellence when they are not swayed by the changes of culture, rather they are embracing the truth found in the Gospel. Excellence is

---

† I guess technically I did what I said I wasn't going to by giving you a list of 10 things here.

standing firm on what Jesus proclaimed no matter what the cost. Being different is being a disciple.

Earlier in this book I mentioned my friend Kevin. If an outsider were to come to Millikin and observe the student body, within a day they would identify Kevin to be different from most individuals. While Kevin still must deal with the pressures and stresses college produces, he is set apart from his peers because of the way he acts.

Very rarely will you see Kevin without a smile for he has a genuine sense of joy within him. And while you might see Kevin out at a party on Saturday night, he is there because he wants to care for those who might not be able to care for themselves. Kevin is loving to every single person he encounters because he realizes life is rough on everyone.

Kevin is not your typical college male, but if you ask me, Kevin is easily one of the most respected individuals at Millikin University. Why? Because he sought to be different.

A mutual friend of Kevin and mine once said, "I am not a huge fan of Christians. They are always trying to push their faith on me and are so judgmental. Not to mention they are hypocrites. But then I met Kevin. He definitely has changed my opinion on what a Christian can be."

Not only was Kevin seeking to be different from what was expected of him as a college student, but he sought to be different from how he thought Christians have become perceived. This is what we all have been called to do. We have been called to defy expectations and become like our Christ.

The night is almost gone; the day of salvation will soon be here. So remove your dark deeds like dirty clothes, and put on the shining armor of right living. Because we belong to the day, we must live decent lives for all to see. Don't participate in the darkness of wild parties and drunkenness, or in sexual promiscuity and immoral living, or in quarreling and jealousy. Instead, clothe yourself with the presence of the Lord Jesus Christ. And don't let yourself think about ways to indulge your evil desires.

Romans 13:12-14

Let us become vessel God uses to change society instead of letting society change us. Let us seek an eternal party in Heaven rather than a short-lived one here. Let us make the decision to be different from those around us by boldly pursuing God's purpose in our lives.

◊ ◊ ◊ ◊ ◊

Often times in Scripture, I come across peculiar passages that cause me to pause and scratch my head. Some of these strange stories I am unable to reason myself to their meaning. Others leave me awestruck. The lesson of boldness in 2 Kings 7 is just one such a story that left me amazed...

The capital city of Israel at the time of this passage was experiencing one of the greatest famines the land had ever seen. This famine however was not brought upon by natural disasters, but due to the Aramean army besieging the city. In chapter 6, we see the severity of the shortage cause by the siege:

The siege lasted so long that a donkey's head sold for eighty pieces of silver, and a cup of dove's dung sold for five pieces of silver.

One day as the king of Israel was walking along the wall of the city, a woman called to him, "Please help me, my lord the king!"

He answered, "If the Lord doesn't help you, what can I do? I have neither food from the threshing floor nor wine from the press to give you." But then the king asked, "What is the matter?"

She replied, "This woman said to me: 'Come on, let's eat your son today, then we will eat my son tomorrow.' So we cooked my son and ate him. Then the next day I said to her, 'Kill your son so we can eat him,' but she has hidden her son."

2 Kings 6:25-29‡

Ordinary citizens within the city were turning to violence, looting, and as seen above, even turning to cannibalism. Food was difficult to come by not just for the poor, but for the wealthy as well. And if this was the situation within walls of the city, imagine what life was like for the outcasts forced to live just outside the city gates. Needless to say, the story of 2 Kings 7 tells of four such individuals. And they were about to prove the adage "desperate times calls for desperate measures" to be true. But through their actions, we are revealed what boldness looks like.

Now there were four men with leprosy sitting at the entrance of the city gates. "Why should we sit here waiting to die?" they asked each other. "We will starve if we stay here, but with the famine in the city, we will starve if we go back there. So we might as well go out and surrender

---

‡ I warned you above this was a strange story.

to the Aramean army. If they let us live, so much the better. But if they kill us, we would have died anyway."

So at twilight they set out for the camp of the Arameans. But when they came to the edge of the camp, no one was there! For the Lord had caused the Aramean army to hear the clatter of speeding chariots and the galloping of horses and the sounds of a great army approaching. "The king of Israel has hired the Hittites and Egyptians to attack us!" they cried to one another. So they panicked and ran into the night, abandoning their tents, horses, donkeys, and everything else, as they fled for their lives.

When the lepers arrived at the edge of the camp, they went into one tent after another, eating and drinking wine; and they carried off silver and gold and clothing and hid it. Finally, they said to each other, "This is not right. This is a day of good news, and we aren't sharing it with anyone! If we wait until morning, some calamity will certainly fall upon us. Come on, let's go back and tell the people at the palace."

2 Kings 7:3-9

Four lepers were so desperate for food they concluded that it would be best to travel to the enemy army camp and beg for table scraps. If the Arameans spared them and fed them as prisoners, they would live. If not, they would die. Seems like a great gamble until you recognize if these men did nothing, they were going to starve anyway. Therefore, they journeyed to the camp because they recognized they had nothing to lose.

What happened when they arrived at the camp? The men discovered the entire enemy had fled for the Lord made the approach of four sound like the attack of thousands. Fearing for their lives, the enemy did not bother to pack up camp before running away, thus leaving a feast for these pariahs of society to indulge upon. There were so many supplies that these men decided to go back to the city and share this great news.

These lepers, who society had turned its back on, decided to go to the people that cast them out and revealed this amazing gift they stumbled upon. They owed nothing to anyone and could have easily kept the spoils of war to themselves, but instead they sought to proclaim the good news with everyone. But what does this story mean for us?

The mentality the lepers had should be the same we possess. We should be living in such a manner where we truly believe we have nothing to lose. Staying in the same place spiritually in life (or staying comfortable in our walks), will ultimately result in the death of our faith. It will result in a spiritual desert plateau to use the geographical language from earlier. Our mission as followers of Christ means going out into the world and taking risks to further the Kingdom of Heaven.

We are called to take the Good News to those who have cast us out of society. We are called to serve those who wish to do us harm. We are called to love those who seek our downfall. I mean, what do we have to lose? Our reputation? Our friends? Our possessions?

Guess what! The world already looks down upon many Christians, so your reputation is already lost... God values His relationship with your friends over your friendship with them so stop idolizing that... and worldly possessions will disappear not to mention we are to store up treasures in Heaven. So really, what do we have to lose?

God has promised (and already achieved) victory, therefore let us stop living as if we are losing the battle, trembling in fear. Rather let us rejoice in the power of the Lord and take risks to proclaim the Message we have been gifted. Our God has gone before us and cleared out the Arameans so that we might truly reside in the promises of Scripture. God will soften the hearts of those who have dismissed you in order for great glory to be shared.

Finally, take notice of this – God used the unclean lepers to do His work. While these men were still filthy and unworthy, God used them. God will still use you despite your past, your struggles, or your sin.

Therefore, be bold messengers, be courageous disciples, be lovers of the broken, be intentional prayer warriors, be righteous risk takers, and above all be true servants of our Lord Jesus Christ. Go all in for Christ even if people call you crazy for doing so. Because odds are, they are just wishing they had the guts to believe in something as much as you do. So, I ask you once more – what do we have to lose?

◊ ◊ ◊ ◊ ◊

All of us have been given various gifts and abilities. And with these gifts, we have the opportunity to faithfully use them in order to point people to Jesus. As seen in the Parable of Talents (Matthew 25:14-30), the Lord has trusted us with a variety of talents we can use to bring Him glory. Some of us might have been entrusted with many talents, and some only a few. Whatever the case though, what matters most is that we are using what the Lord has given us.

If we sit on the knowledge we have been given, then we are showing our unfaithfulness. If we are only giving partial effort towards the things we are doing, we reveal a lack of desire to fulfill God's plan in our lives. If we decide to do the bare minimum in our spiritual journey, then we might find ourselves to be in some serious trouble the day the Lord calls us home.

One of my basketball coaches at Millikin often shares with the team a motto that illustrates this point well. It is three simple words but speaks volumes towards what is expected of us in all things... "Fill your cup." God has given each of us a cup to fill in our lives. Those who He has given much might be said to have a gallon-sized cup, while those who have been given little might only have a Dixie cup. What matters most however, is not the size of the cup we have been given, but how full our cup is.§

When we decide to be the best student, employee, mom, dad, athlete, musician, or friend we can be, that is the moment our cup becomes full. When we step out in faith and heed the words of Colossians 3:17 (NIV), our cup will overflow.

And whatever you do, whether in word or deed,
do it all in the name of the Lord Jesus, giving
thanks to God the Father through him.

Will there be moments we fail to fill our cups? Of course. Will there be situations we sabotage our own cup by poking holes in it? Most definitely. Thankfully, this is where grace comes into the picture.

God knows at points fear will overcome our faith and doubt will overshadow our ability to trust in Him. But because we serve a gracious and forgiving Lord who came

---

§ My coach, Kramer Soderberg, was in the process of publishing a book called *Fill Your Cup for Christ* as I was writing this chapter. My hope and prayer are that by the time this book finds itself into your hands, his book has touch thousands of lives for the sake of Christ.

down to Earth in the form of a man, died a painful death in our place, and rose from the grave defeating Hell in the process, we can be assured of a second chance to fill our cup. And a third chance... and a fourth... and a fifth... need I continue?

Does this grace mean we should no longer seek to develop our faith and fill our cup? By no means! We seek excellence in our faith journey when we strive to do good in all things. We do not wish abuse grace's effects (Romans 6:1-2). Let us live in a manner as if grace did not exist, but at the same time let us be thankful that it does. Let our faith be grown by our actions, and let grace mold this growth into that which is pleasing to the Lord. This, I believe, is truly excellent.

◊ ◊ ◊ ◊ ◊

Pursuing excellence begins with making the decision to *be different* from the world around you. It develops as you choose to *go boldly* into the world and share the Message you have been given. And it has reached its pinnacle when declare you will *remain faithful* through whatever this world throws at you. Doing these things might be easy on the mountain where we feel close to God and in the valley where we must trust fully on God. But the real test of excellence is measured when the pressure is off.

When we are not on a spiritual high or low, will we forget God and return to old ways? Or will we seek to develop a deeper, genuine faith in Christ? During all seasons in life, we must commit to be growing closer to our Father.

We serve a perfect Lord who seeks us to be perfect – something we are incapable of achieving by ourselves. But as legendary football coach Vince Lombardi once said, "Perfection is unattainable, but if we chase perfection, we can catch excellence." And this sentiment is echoed in Philippians 3:12 (CSB):

> *Not that I have already reached the goal or am already perfect, but I make every effort to take hold of it because I also have been taken hold of by Christ Jesus.*

If there is one thing I hope you have taken from this book, it is the idea of surrender seen in the second half of this verse. Only when we let Christ have complete hold of our lives can any of the topics I have discussed fully be implemented. We cannot be perfect, but we can allow our perfect Savior to live through us. This command is simple to understand, but as I have said countless times before this point – it is not easy to do. For excellent things are not often gained without having to overcome a mountainous terrain.

Ryan's Story

I spent my high school and early college years longing for approval from my family, peers, and God. I thought if I could just find myself approved by others, I could have a truly fulfilling life. And I convinced myself I could achieve a 'perfect life' on my own. For in my head, all I had to do was be a good enough guy to obtain that life. So being Christian was simply a means to that end because I thought being Christian meant I only had to partake in Christian things. Going to church, reading Scripture, and occasionally attending a Bible study were all things that were going to win me the approval I sought.

With the longing for this approval being a driving force of my life, I decided to search for the perfect life in partying and relationships. These actions would make me approved by man and the Christians things I did would help me meet the qualifications for God. As time passed though, one feeling continued to overcome me repeatedly. That feeling was of guilt and purposelessness.

The life I was living felt great in the moment, but why would I feel so unsatisfied when I awoke in the morning? Was this all the perfect life really had to offer? Everything the world was telling me to do, I did yet I never found fulfillment. Was this truly all that the world had to offer?

But then I began observing the life of those around me who were faithfully pursuing Christ. And yeah, despite me doing those Christian things, my life looked nothing like theirs. They possessed a desire to know the Lord; a love for life that I never really felt. How could they experience life like that? What did they have that I was missing? While I was not entirely sure what I needed to do, I knew something wasn't right and my life needed a sturdier foundation.

Day by day I took little steps of pursuing the true message of the Gospel though Scripture and conversations with faithful followers of Jesus. And from those things I realized for the first time that I am simply not good... like at all. No matter how hard I tried I could never live this perfect life that my heart so truly desired. I myself never measured up to the way I viewed perfection – the way I sought excellence.

But thankfully I did not have to measure up by myself. I had the ability to join into Someone's story who does measure up. The perfect life of Jesus Christ and His glorious message of the cross is more than enough. So when I learned I was not enough, the message of the Gospel begun to truly take root in my life. Something I heard hundreds of times took on a new role in guiding how I lived. For because of the cross and the grace of God, my name and life have now been deemed excellent. Not because of anything I have done or can do, but because of the righteous blood of Christ.

As it reads in 2 Corinthians 5:21, *"For God made Christ, who never sinned, to be the offering for our sin, so that we could be made right with God through Christ."* No longer did I have to feel shame and guilt from not living up to my expectation of excellence, but rather I could live knowing that I am actually a part of a Story much greater than my own. And for me, what a privilege it is to be a part of that Story... a part of the excellent and perfect Story of Christ.

-CHAPTER 12-

A STORY YET TO BE WRITTEN

Two thousand years ago, twelve men made a decision to follow an individual on His journey to change the world. They uprooted themselves from the comfort and predictability of their own lives to depart on a mission that would forever alter history. These men would help form and grow a religion that would eventually become the most followed in the world. Twelve individual stories intersected to create the supporting details of one greater Story. Yes, I am obviously referring to the 12 Disciples.

Thomas, Simon the Zealot, Philip, Peter, Matthew, Jude, Judas Iscariot, John, James, Son of Alpheus, James the Son of Zebedee, Bartholomew, and Andrew all were ordinary, young men yet we know their names and their stories today because of who they decided to follow.

There was nothing special about any of these men; most had "blue-collared' jobs and were not the most educated people around. Yet, for some reason they were still chosen by Christ to be used.

Christ intentionally passed over the elite, aristocratic, and influential men of society and chose the men from the lowly parts of society. Just as I wrote back in chapter 1,

Christ here is seen to exalt the humble and put low those who are proud. In layman's terms, Jesus took twelve below average kids from 1st century Palestine and changed the world.

And in changing the world, each disciple had a role to play. They played a role during Christ's earthly ministry and in the early years of building the Church. Even the disciple who would turn his back on his Messiah in betrayal, played an important role in God's ultimate rescue of humanity.

We too have a role to play in God's plan for today. He is calling out to us despite the fact we might view ourselves as vastly underqualified. Well guess what?!? God does not just use pastors, priests, and vocational missionaries to complete His work... He will use you where you are at.

God will use you as a student or a teacher, an intern or a manager, an athlete or a musician, a single mother or a stay at home dad, an addict or a social worker, a farmer or a computer coder, and yes He will even use you if you are a Chicago Cubs fan.* God will use you just as He used the Disciples.

And if you are convinced this is not the case, then ask yourself – why not? Why not let God use you like the Disciples? Why not let your story be the next story of the Twelve? Is He not able to do it again?

I believe I serve a God of the impossible, so why not let Him use my story. Let Him use the parts of my life I try to keep in the shadows in order to reveal His glorious light. Let Him use my weaknesses and insufficiencies to demonstrate His grave-defying power. Let Him use my talents and abilities in a manner His grace and mercy can be on full display. Let Him use me. Let Him use you.

---

* Yes, I am a STL Cardinals fan. Not my fault I like good baseball.

◊ ◊ ◊ ◊ ◊

Throughout the chapters of this book and the topics discussed, I hope you now feel more equipped to take on the challenge and adventure of living out the Christian faith. Furthermore, my prayer is the words I have written are unlike anything you have read before. For I believe while we might be familiar with these topics, it is rare to see their genuine forms show up in our society today. This begins to change now with us.

Living the components of faith will be difficult – it is an everyday battle. Some might try to convince you to be Christian means to follow a 3-step process to find your best life now. Do not let this lie deceive you! As I hope I have demonstrated throughout this book, our faith is to be a vibrant, active, and constantly transforming thing. So why would we ever confine it to be like that of a cookbook recipe? I know God has much more in store for us than that.

I believe God can and will use us to do amazing things for the Kingdom of Heaven. Just as He used the Apostles to teach great lessons and perform even greater miracles, so also God can use us in remarkable ways. He is wanting to use our story as a chapter pointing people to a much greater Story. And as you are reading this, our Lord is already writing the next page of this book called life.

Personally, I am glad to be part of a Story being written by the most creative, dynamic, and alluring teacher to ever walk this earth. That is why I tried to write this book not as if I was presenting a formula to solve a math problem called Christianity, but rather as painting a portrait of the most beautiful truth we can know. Our journey with Christ is not supposed to be dull but should be something that brings life to every room we walk into. When others look at us, they see a Story they want to become part of.

Recognize, we all have a great story needing to be shared. Some of our stories contain many chapters, some might have just begun a few chapters ago. But wherever the status of our stories currently is, let us do our best to make our life stories worth reading.

When looking at the mass majority of the population today, most people will never have a biography written about them for their lives can be defined by the current events and sociology of our time... "So and so grew up, went to college, wasted their education, settled into a job, started a family, quit a job, grew old, died."

Is it just me, or are you convinced life should be much more than that? Because it should be! Our stories should stick out because the main character is the most interesting protagonist ever... and no it is not ourselves.

We must learn the truth many people will never discover. Look back at the Disciples – they did not become the most celebrated people in church history by proclaiming their own name and doing things to make themselves great. They were special because of who they knew, not what they did.

In fact, take out Jesus, and the Disciples can easily be defined by the history of their time. Only with Jesus did their lives become accounts worth of study. Only through Jesus did their life story have any meaning. And the same can be true for us.

While our goal should not be personal fame, we still should stick out from the crowd. People should look at us and want to know our story because of how different we are. And the reason we are different is due to the fact we have surrendered control of our lives to the hand of Christ.

After all, our stories by themselves mean nothing. But with Christ, they become testimonies of God's power and grace at work in our world today. They become tools to be used to bring glory to the Father and to make His name known.

But let us be honest – sometimes in life, we lose track of the fact God wants us to be a part of a larger Story because our life is not going so well. And if you are anything like me (or like anyone I wrote about throughout the first 11 chapters of this book), you will struggle to believe in the role we can play in God's plans. Doubt will exist.

Even Paul, the author of most of the New Testament, at points struggled. And this was a man who was literally blinded by the goodness of God! But at the end of the day, we recognize Paul as a man who remained faithful.

How can we be like Paul? How can we remain faithful in our story despite how wrong it might seem to be going? For even if we have had a Road to Damascus experience like Paul (ref. Acts 9) where we have been completely over-whelmed by the presence of God, let us not be naïve in our thinking that we will never struggle with our faith.

Yes, it is true for some, one miraculous Damascus moment will be all they need to walk faithfully every day after. But others will need a dozen Damascus' for God to fully become real to them. More often than not though, we might just need a simple reminder of who Jesus is when we get off track rather than a Damascus-level experience. This is where the Road to Emmaus enters our stories.

Immediately following the Resurrection of Jesus, we read this account in Luke 24:13-33:

> *That same day two of Jesus' followers were walking to the village of Emmaus, seven miles from Jerusalem. As they walked along they were talking about everything that had happened. As they talked and discussed these things, Jesus himself suddenly came and began*

walking with them. But God kept them from recognizing him.

He asked them, "What are you discussing so intently as you walk along?"

They stopped short, sadness written across their faces. Then one of them, Cleopas, replied, "You must be the only person in Jerusalem who hasn't heard about all the things that have happened there the last few days."

"What things?" Jesus asked.

"The things that happened to Jesus, the man from Nazareth," they said. "He was a prophet who did powerful miracles, and he was a mighty teacher in the eyes of God and all the people. But our leading priests and other religious leaders handed him over to be condemned to death, and they crucified him. We had hoped he was the Messiah who had come to rescue Israel. This all happened three days ago.

"Then some women from our group of his followers were at his tomb early this morning, and they came back with an amazing report. They said his body was missing, and they had seen angels who told them Jesus is alive! Some of our men ran out to see, and sure enough, his body was gone, just as the women had said."

Then Jesus said to them, "You foolish people! You find it so hard to believe all that the prophets wrote in the Scriptures. Wasn't it clearly predicted that the Messiah would have to suffer all these things before entering his glory?" Then Jesus took them through the writings of Moses and all the prophets, explaining from all the Scriptures the things concerning himself.

By this time they were nearing Emmaus and the end of their journey. Jesus acted as if he were going on, but they begged him, "Stay the night with us, since it is getting late." So he went home with them. As they sat down to eat, he took the bread and blessed it. Then he broke it and gave it to them. Suddenly, their eyes were opened, and they recognized him. And at that moment he disappeared!

They said to each other, "Didn't our hearts burn within us as he talked with us on the road and explained the Scriptures to us?" And within the hour they were on their way back to Jerusalem.

These two disciples were blinded by their expectations and current circumstances to remember the promises that Jesus had taught during His ministry. So what does Jesus do? He gives them a recap of everything that has happened so far. He reminds them that everything has occurred according to what the Scriptures had declared. And what do they do? They sprint back to Jerusalem to reunite with the other disciples, eager to share the Good News they have witnessed.

So for us, when we lose track of our story – our purpose, our mission, our hope – let us allow Christ to give the recap and then let's run off to continue creating the next chapter. Let us make the decision to act upon the lessons we have learned up to this point.

Let us act in *humility* allowing God to receive all the glory.

Let us be people of *integrity* by practicing what we preach.

Let us seek *transformation*, keeping our hearts open to encounters with God.

Let us fulfill God's *purpose* in our lives no matter what the cost.

Let us live with *authenticity*, not fearing rejection of man.

Let us lead a life of *prayer*, searching for wisdom from above.

Let us show the same type of *love* to others Christ has shown us.

Let us serve our peers by striving to *sacrifice* our own comfort.

Let us pursue fellowship through *companionship* with other believers.

Let us have a sense of *urgency*, using our time to its greatest potential.

Let us become men and women seeking *excellence* in all.

And one day when our story reaches the final page, what will happen? Hopefully for everyone reading this, we will start a new book, namely one titled *"An Eternity in Heaven."* But past that, I pray a new chapter begins here on earth because the main character in our life lives on. We will not fall to the trap of placing so high a value in protecting our legacy that we get in the way of God. Instead, we will allow Him to use our story as a catalyst to begin the first chapter of the greater Story in our friends and family around us.

Today, let us decide to make the Story of Christ so obvious in our lives that people see us as a character that just jumped out of the Bible. When our story ends, let hell throw a party for we are no longer in the fight... but let that party be short lived for our enemy will realize that we left behind a powerful message of Good News in our absence.

When our story ends, let us have the confidence to boldly declare the same sentiment Paul declared at the end of his life:

*I have fought the good fight, I have finished the race, and **I have remained faithful**.*

2 Timothy 4:7

Even though the fight might have been tough, and I might have been knocked down many times... Even though the race might have been long, and I might have had to limp through much of it... Even though this life has tried to get me to give up on God... I have remained faithful.

This is a bold declaration that I hope we all can affirm at the end of our journey. But in the meantime, let us work on *remaining* faithful. Whatever stage of life you find yourself in – high school, college, starting a family, finding your first job, or about to retire to Florida – work to remain faithful in everything. Give Christ complete control over your life and watch what your story will become.

Give Him the pen within your heart and let Him create your life into a story worthy to be shouted from rooftops. Not because your story is so special, but because Christ can be clearly observed through your story. And no matter what your past has held, keep progressing through your story. Stop living in the past and start allowing Christ to live through your todays. For as C.S. Lewis so excellently wrote, "You can't go back and change the beginning, but you can start where you are and change the ending."

As you close this book, I pray the story of your life opens to a new chapter. One marked by traits of humility, integrity, and love. One set on glorifying our Creator in every step we take and breath we breathe. One that embraces the message of the Gospel by living it and proclaiming it. Above all, I pray what follows from here is a chapter penned by an Author other than ourselves...

And from this Author I leave you with some final words taken from the Book where we can most clearly see hundreds of stories interwoven together to tell the Greatest Story of all time. From the Maker of all Creation and the Author of our Salvation comes a remarkable call to action and reminder of purpose. Pay close attention to it... strive to live in it... rejoice because of it!

May the grace of the Lord Jesus be with all. Amen.†

---

† From Revelation 22:21 (ESV).

YOUR STORY

Following each chapter of this book were various stories of individuals who found their lives to be small parts of the Larger Story of Christ. When I began the journey writing this book, I knew that the addition of these stories would be vital. For I recognized that no matter how well I wrote or what parts of my life story I told, I was not going to be able to directly speak to each person who read my book. But allowing this book to become a platform for others to tell parts of their story might just be what makes this book special.

I asked some of my brothers and sisters in Christ to write stories which pertained to the themes I discussed in my own writing. With very little instruction as to what these stories were to look like, I entrusted them with perhaps the most important task of this project. I did not give them many guidelines because I was seeking to have them tell their story unhindered (except for a brief rule of a word limit). Each story came out very different from the next and that was exactly what I sought. For our faith journey is not a formula to follow but it is an adventure we get to take part in.

And like me, the writers of the stories in this book are not overly special in any way. All of us were either in college of just out of college when we wrote what we did. However, the testimonies provided are extremely special because they show what it looks like to surrender authorship to the Lord.

God has asked each and every one of us to participate in this great Story He is telling. We have each been given a different role and have various tasks to complete. But one thing each of our stories is capable of achieving is helping point others to the Gospel message... the Story of Scripture. From an embarrassing moment that teaches a lesson of humility to an inspirational tale showing the power of prayer, small pieces of our lives are able to contribute to the mosaic masterpiece of our Messiah. This was the reason I deemed it necessary to include as many stories from other believers as possible.

But what of this last story? And didn't I end the book already with a final "amen?" To which I respond as such – I feel it was my responsibility to keep the ending of this book open-ended. This way you as a reader knows that the greater Story I have discussed itself is not yet over. Better yet, each of you reading and me writing have the privilege to take in the Story that is still spreading to this day. Until God places the final period on our world's narrative, the journey goes on.

For this reason, I invite every person who has made it to the conclusion of this book to share with me the stories of their lives in Christ. This last story, the twelfth story, has been reserved for you. This one is yours to fill in. So I challenge you to reach out to me and let me know how God has been working in your life. Email your story to My12thStory@gmail.com and I look forward to being encouraged by you as hopefully you were encouraged by me.

Let us write this next chapter hand and hand with each other and Christ. Let us see our world changed one story at a time.

ACKNOWLEDGEMENTS

Before all else, I would like to thank my family for their unwavering support of me over the years. I know whatever endeavor I set out on they are going to have my back which made the challenge of publishing a book so much easier. Thank you for all the lessons and stories you all have taught me... much of the material in this book was heavily influenced by each of you (especially the puns).

A huge thank you goes out to the guys at Millikin who I had the privilege to be in community with during my 4 years at college. Our endless discussions about all things sports, classes, and Jesus kept me grounded during this long writing journey.

To my 11 brothers and sisters in Christ who took time out of their busy schedules to write the stories for in between each chapter, I cannot even begin to express how much I appreciate you all! Your willingness to share your stories elevated this book to a level I never would have imagined!

To the James Millikin Scholar Program, thank you for giving me the opportunity to pursue this ambitious idea for my Senior Honor's project. The research I was able to conduct through this program ultimately gave me the motivation and drive to see this book through to its conclusion.

Finally, to everyone who encouraged me, inspired me, and prayed for me as I wrote this book – thank you! My story is all the better because of each of you.

Made in the USA
Monee, IL
10 December 2023

47818262R00115